The One Inside

30 Days to Your *Authentic Self*

Tammy Sollenberger, M.A.

For press inquiries, contact the author at
Blue Cottage Agency
krista@bluecottageagency.com

First edition December 2021
Third Printing
Printed in the United States of America

Published by
Pure Carbon Publishing
an Imprint of Living Your Dream, LLC
Glendale, AZ
www.purecarbonpublishing.com

ISBN: 978-0-9676887-5-6
EPUB ISBN: 978-0-9676887-6-3
Library of Congress Control Number: 2021948705

Edited and Designed by The Story Laboratory
Editor: Kelly Lydick
Interior Design: Tabitha Lahr
www.writeeditdesignlab.com

To Aris.
The One Inside of you lights up the One Inside of me.

 Contents

Phase Three: Healing

PROLOGUE · *Harmony*

I became a therapist because I have always been fascinated with people. To be honest I am a bit nosey, and I love people's stories. But I really do love helping people. I love being a part of the process that helps each person live their best life, to feel their best. I love seeing people succeed in their relationships and goals. I love helping people get out of those stuck places that seem to hold them back. I love helping people win in whatever area they desire.

And, for a time, I was doing that. I was working as a licensed therapist in a group therapy practice and doing what I had been trained to do. I was trying to help people challenge their thoughts, debate with their beliefs, and question their actions.

It was fine. It was ok. I was helping. I was building rapport. I was . . . fine.

But on an usually bright, sunny day—one of the first of the season—in New England, I attended a child therapy workshop with a friend. I don't see children in my practice so I was really there to support my friend and learn a bit. When the speaker turned out to be boring and the sun was shining through the windows, I was beside myself with regret.

We cherish warm, sunny days where I live. We get at least six months of winter so when the sun starts shining, most people come out of their caves of dark slumber, blinking their eyes to adjust to the light, and bask it all of the sun's glory. I did the same, just staying there soaking in the sun's warmth.

But I was still grumpy. I found myself thinking: "I'm sitting in this stupid room, at this stupid workshop. Why am I here?"

Then, I heard the speaker say something about a new therapy that was becoming popular in Boston. This piqued my interest. I like new things! I definitely like to know what the popular things are. I perked up.

She said, "What if we were curious about our client's parts?"

That was it.

My internal dialogue sounded something like, "Wait. I wonder what it would be like to be curious about why they do the thing that they do not want to do? I wonder what it would feel like to be curious about why they stay in relationships, why they act in ways they regret, why they say horrible things to themselves?"

I was used to fixing, changing, blaming, shaming. I was used to being intellectual and analyzing. I treated my clients this way and I treated myself this way, too.

She also said this thing about parts. Ok, so what if I thought it was just a part of the client who did the thing, said the thing, acted this way, believed this way?

That. Made. So. Much. Sense.

As I sat there, I felt what I would later call a "soft curiosity," and I noticed how different that felt in my body and in my head. It certainly shifted me out of my grumpy state.

I continued to consider this idea of having a soft curiosity toward and with my clients. What if I invited them to have a soft curiosity, too? What if I also started to have a soft curiosity toward myself?

And, this changed everything for me, for my practice, for my clients—and for my life.

I went back to my office, forgetting the beautiful day in front of me, and googled this new model called Internal Family Systems (or IFS) and found out it had been around almost 30 years. This model of therapy that invited me to be curious was not new, it would soon be evidence based, making it able to stand alongside the traditional models I had been trained in.

Later that summer, I attended a weeklong workshop with the founder, Richard Schwartz. I began my own IFS therapy as was highly recommended. I read every book about IFS that I could get my hands on. I attended all the one-day workshops. I found out there was a group working hard to get a training in Maine, so I attended all of that group's pre-training events. We were fortunate to get that training, and I completed a year-long level one training. Then I worked as a staff member at a level one training and completed a level two training. Then I worked as a staff member at a level two. I did a workshop at the annual conference to help those beginning to learn the model. I started an IFS podcast.

I do not want anyone to be stuck in outdated, sometimes unhelpful therapy. I do not want them doing it, and I do not want them receiving it.

There is a better way.

I am passionate about helping people feel reinvigorated in the way they do therapy and get therapy. I want to help people understand themselves, to get to know themselves in a new way with compassion and kindness.

IFS changed me. It changed how I facilitate the therapeutic process. It changed how I see people and how I see myself.

I want to invite you to have a soft curiosity, the kind that comes from your heart and not your head.

The process of the next 30 days is going to be unlike anything you have done before. This is not your typical self-help book. It is not the same old, same old book about self-awareness that you have read before.

In order to help you create inner harmony in a more radical way than ever before, I'll provide a step-by-step process that can be explored and completed in small digestible pieces. I am going to walk you through how to experience this way of thinking and being and feeling. Together, through these pages, we will dig in with soft curiosity, with compassion, and with kindness.

This process has the potential to change everything.

I'd like to start our journey together by sharing a little bit of inner dialogue I noticed inside of me the other day. It sounded like this:

"Why can't you get yourself together?" I asked myself several times a day. That question was followed by, "You need to do better. What is wrong with you?"

I looked around the room. Who was this voice speaking to? Oh, it was me. I am talking to myself. The type of inner chatter I experience typically sounds similar.

I am upset because I forgot to fill out a school form. Or, I do not want to get out of bed, and I have a full day of clients. Or, I am standing at the kitchen counter shoving chocolate chip cookies into my mouth.

This inner self talk is constant and ever changing.

Sometimes I just hear commentary: "Oh that is a pretty house. Maybe you should paint your front door that color yellow. Is that canary yellow?"

Sometimes it is a bit more menacing: "Are you ever going to get your eating under control? You are really ridiculous. Why do you bother exercising if you are going to eat this way?"

Often it isn't a voice but a completely different way of acting and speaking who does not feel like my 40-ish year old "me." I stomp my feet on my way out of the room shouting, "Fine. Do whatever you want!" when my 10-year-old says he does not want to stop playing video games.

Sometimes it's a version of myself that I don't recognize. My friend says she wants to go out to eat when I had told her I wanted to go to the paint your own picture place. I smile and say, "Sure" and am cold and distant and only answer in one word phrases all night. Another voice says to me, "Snap out of it, weirdo!"

Sometimes it feels like a younger version of me. My mom comes to visit, and she tells me as nicely as possible that I have put my window curtain on wrong. I act like I don't hear her. Or, I roll my eyes and tell her I wanted it that way. Or, I make myself as small as possible and say, "I'm so sorry. Show me how to do it. Actually, I'll just do it wrong, so can you do it for me?"

At times I am too sensitive. At times I can't access emotions at all. At times I feel like I like an angsty 13-year-old. At times I just want to snuggle with one of my son's teddy bears and hide under a blanket. At times I am hurried, rushed, and overextended. At times I can't get off the couch and cannot imagine leaving the house ever.

At times I am grounded, calm and feel like. . . . Me.

What is happening? Why do I have so much chatter in my head? Why do I act in ways I don't like? Why do I self-sabotage myself over and over again?

What would it feel like to lean into these voices with curiosity? What else would they tell me? I wonder what it would feel like if they were softer, if they felt like my greatest helpers, and my favorite encouragers? I wonder what it would feel like if I believed they were on my side and in my corner?

I wonder what it would feel like if "I" was more present to these voices, to these versions of myself so they did not play tug of war with my mind and my body. I wonder what it would be like if The One Inside had a bit more leadership with all of the parts of me. I wonder if "I" listen to these parts, they may teach me something about myself.

Begin to separate the idea that parts are all of you. You are an "I" and you have parts. There is the "Me" and there are many parts. We call the I, "Self." When you read below "You," I am beginning to help you shift into this way of thinking. Imagine if YOU thought and felt this way about your parts.

Imagine what it would be like if you became curious about the parts of you who wall yourself off to others and to your feelings. Imagine if you were curious about your highly driven and perfectionistic parts. Imagine if you were curious about the critical parts who judge you so harshly. Imagine if you were curious about your anxious parts, your sad parts, your angry parts, your addicted parts.

What if we began to think of these symptoms, these qualities of personality, and these attributes that are in the way of our harmony and happiness as varying parts of us? These parts of us who have a purpose, a positive intention, and a plan to help.

You may think, "Wait. These bad parts of me do not have good intentions. They make things worse for me, not better."

One of the assertions of the IFS model is that all parts of you are trying to help you in their own way. They have one idea of how to help and they stick to this idea, not knowing that it may cost you in other ways, particularly if other parts are not in agreement or aligned.

What if we were open to what these parts wanted to tell us instead of trying to change them or make them go away? What if we started a dialogue with them to bring them into better harmony? Here is an example of me trying to get to know my "wall" part, the part of me who keeps me emotionally numb and distant from others:

ME (THE SELF): *Hi, Wall. I am curious about you. How are you trying to help me?*

WALL: *If I am not here people will hurt you. You let people too close, too soon.*

ME: *Oh, yes. There are other parts who do that, who can be too trusting. You keep the good and the bad out, though.*

WALL: *I don't care. I need to keep the bad out. I never want us to hurt again.*

ME: *Makes sense. I understand. When did you start doing this? When did it become so important to keep the bad out?*

WALL: *When we were little and changed schools. We were afraid nobody would like us and the other kids did not accept us at first.*

ME: *What if we can go to the little girl part of me inside who experienced that and help her? What if we can let her know that is no longer happening? Would you be interested in trying that?*

WALL: *Possibly.*

I know this may sound *very* weird. I get that. I also want to say it is *not* weird because we all have dialogues going on inside. All. Day. Long. This idea also can explain why we have intense feelings about something in the now based on an experience we had in the past.

Imagine that you could help this little girl who changed schools so the wall who is protecting her does not have to work so hard. With your wall part more flexible, you could show up differently in your current relationships.

We do not try to get rid of the wall, to get rid of any of our protective parts; we want to help them shift from their extreme roles. We do this by helping and healing what and who inside they are protecting; the younger parts who are stuck in the past in a place of pain and isolation.

Creating Your Own Harmony

As you read about the wall part did a memory or similar personal experience come to mind? Do you have parts who resonated with this or responded with a story of their own? What did you notice happening inside of you as you read it?

I want to invite you to take a minute of two to lean into your own experience right now. What are you hearing? What are you experiencing as you have read this so far? I suggest writing down what is happening inside of you right now—the phrases you are hearing in your mind, any feelings, or bodily sensations.

Now, I want you to start to notice the times you say or think, "A part of me thinks/wants/feels such and such." My guess is that this is familiar, and you are probably not used to interacting with these "parts" as I did above.

Listening inside, noticing parts, beginning to interact with parts is a first step down the road towards harmony. Disharmony is the experience of wrestling with yourself internally. For example, a part of me thinks I should take a job, another part of me is afraid so it says I should not take a job, and another part wants to eat all the cookies because I am overwhelmed and unsure. Lots of my parts want cookies!

Note a few ways you experience disharmony, the tug of war, back and forth in your mind. You will get to know these parts as you continue on this journey.

This internal connection creates harmony. Here are a few synonyms for harmony that capture what I want to experience in my heart, mind, and body. It is the way I want to feel toward all the parts of me. Notice the reactions you have to these words:

- Consensus
- Cooperation
- Unity
- Accord
- Friendship
- Rapport
- Goodwill
- Kinship
- Understanding
- Concord

- Affinity
- Like minded
- Meeting of the minds

Imagine if you have these feelings amongst the parts of you, amongst the voices, opinions, sensations, thoughts inside of you. What a difference this would make in your overall well-being, your actions, and in your relationships with others.

The Internal Family Systems (IFS) Model

The Internal Family Systems Model of psychotherapy was founded by Dr. Richard Schwartz over thirty years ago. Dick tells the story of when he was working with clients with eating disorders, he noticed they talked about the parts of themselves; parts who wanted to lose weight and parts who wanted to stop binging and purging. He also discovered that when the client would speak in a calmer tone, he would ask, "Who is that part?" and they would say, "That is just me."

Dick realized that not only do these clients have parts, but he did, too. He gathered a group of other curious seekers around him who helped him develop the IFS model. IFS became another major model of psychotherapy and an evidence-based practice of psychotherapy.

IFS is not just an evidenced based therapeutic model; it is a way of thinking about the personality and the mind. It is now being used in schools and businesses. It integrated in 12-step programs and inside prisons.

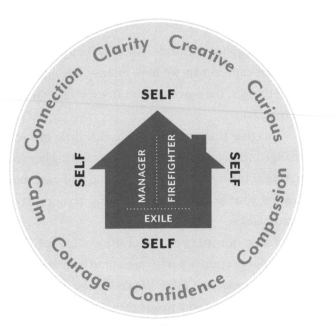

These are terms used throughout the book and will be explained in much more detail as you move along this journey.

The System:

SELF: The true essence we each have. Self has qualities such as calm, centered, creative, courageous, clear-minded, and curious. It is our "heart- mind," our soul, the center of our being. Many spiritual traditions have names for this One inside of us.

PARTS: These are sub-personalities who drive the bus of our lives. They protect us or they need protecting. They always have good intentions and our ultimate safety in mind.

MANAGERS: This is one type of protector. It anticipates problems and acts to make sure we do not have to deal with them. It is proactive and organized. It is the thinking, figure-it-out leader in our system.

 FIREFIGHTERS: This is another type of protector. It is reactive and impulsive It can be addictive, a trouble maker, and are often not liked by other parts.

 EXILES: These are the parts who need protecting. They are younger, vulnerable, parts of us who often hold burdens and big feelings. They are stuck in "the basement" so we are not influenced, flooded, or overwhelmed by their feelings. We are often not aware they are even there.

Terms we use to help and work with our system:

UNBLEND: This is the term to describe the skill of separating out parts from Self. We are "blended" with parts all the time. Unblending helps the "You" have space from the "Part."

TARGET PART: The part we are focused on getting to know. It helps us have a focus as other parts may have opinions about this part. It helps to keep the target in the center of our awareness.

TRAILHEAD: A trigger. A sign that leads us down a path to get to know our parts.

UNBURDEN: Parts carry burdens from the hard things they have been through. Unburdening is a process in IFS to heal our parts from the burdens they carry. Burdens can be thoughts, beliefs, and feelings.

What does "internal family" mean? Let's say we have a traditional family of a mother, father, sister and brother. In all families, like in all types of relationships, there is a way of being with one another, a dance.

Here's an example of a **family dance**: The father comes home from work tired and hungry. The mother anxiously anticipates this and diligently arranges her appearance, cleans the house, and has a plate of food prepared. The sister picks out her favorite art project to show him and make sure she has cleaned her face and hands. She sits quietly waiting for her dad and does not want to upset her mom. The brother refuses to participate in this game. He knows they think he is the problem. He got in trouble at school today and does not care. He will be the object of dad's anger at dinner and the reason they all end up upset at the end of the night.

This was their dance, their family system: mom and sister walking on eggshells around father, the father and brother at odds. They all responded and reacted to one another. They all anticipated one another's moods and behaviors.

If we wanted to get to know one member of this family, it would make sense to ask the other members to wait in another room. We would also want to show curious attention and interest in that person. We do not want to have any favorites. We would ask questions, knowing that their feelings and behaviors makes sense to them inside this system.

We all have an internal system and just like an external system, all parts play a role. Parts of us relate to one another. Parts of us anticipate needs. Parts of us react to upsetting things.

Internal Family Systems is a way of thinking about our personality facets and how they function as a whole and in parts. It is a framework of getting to know the parts of us who make us who we are, the parts of us who try to protect us and the parts of us who need protecting. We also have, this adult leader in our system who is called our Self. This Self is the inner core essence of who we are.

Harmony occurs in our individual system when the Self is the leader and all the parts have connection and access to Self. Harmony occurs when the parts look to the Self and not just react and respond to one another. Harmony occurs when the protective parts trust the Self to take care of the parts who need protecting.

Not only does harmony occur, but healing also occurs. Healing of depression. Healing of anxiety. Healing of tension. Healing of pain. Healing of past abuse. Healing of conflictual relationships. Healing of stress and turmoil. Healing in order to be the One we are meant to be.

That is the goal of this book: to help you get to know the parts who make up your internal family, to bring in more leadership by listening and befriending the ones who protect, and to be with and heal the ones who need protecting.

Working with the Parts

Internal Family Systems helps us understand, work with, and heal the conflict going on within, the disharmony we all experience at times.

Parts are your "internal family" and these "family members" inside react to one another. The critic reacts to the shame, the anger reacts to the sadness, and the guilt reacts to the anger, for example.

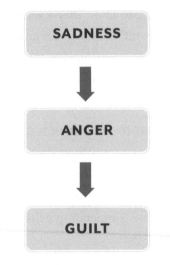

SHAME SAYS: "I'm embarrassed I spoke up in the meeting." I feel sick to my stomach.

THE CRITIC SAYS: "Of course you are embarrassed. Why can't you be more confident? Your co-workers are and they do not know what they are talking about. You are so pathetic."

SADNESS SAYS: "I wish I had a loving partner in my life. I will never have that (or fill in the blank: I wish I had _____ .)"

ANGER SAYS: "Be more grateful for what you do have!"

GUILT SAYS: "I feel bad for wishing things were different. Shame on me for thinking that way. I should be more grateful." I feel small, hunched over, and my head hangs low.

You may think of these parts as your inner voice, or one of your inner voices. Consider the things you tend to say to yourself about yourself. These are your parts.

How to Use This Book

I am excited you have made it this far. IFS is a simple and complex model. My goal and my wish is to simplify this for you one word at a time. This introduction is an overview with a lot of information. Take a deep breath right now. We are going to go on a 30-day journal together, slowing all of this down and engaging with your system one word a day.

Keep a journal with you as you read and carry it with you throughout the day to track your parts. There will be a noticing or awareness exercise every day. I hope you have already started noting some of your parts.

Imagine this as a 30-day intensive class to learn about your own personality, your inner system. I also want to encourage you to listen to your inner knowing. If you need to read ahead, do it. If you need to read one day over and over, do it. I want you to honor what your parts need.

You may have a manager part who tells you differently. You may hear inside, "We *have* to do each word a day. We *should* finish this in 30 days." Let's add this part as one of the first parts you get to know, this part that says there is a "right" way to do something. This is similar to my manager who says adding the word "**harmony**" to the prologue is adding a 31ˢᵗ word.

In the first phase of the book, you will begin mapping your system. You will start to notice who are the major parts and what they sound like and feel like. You will begin to connect to and notice this True Essence, Your **Self**.

Note about the word "Self": Whatever phrase or term works for you here, use it. Some people like authentic Self, true spirit, essence, heart, or soul. Use wording that fits with you and makes sense for your system.

In the second phase, you will start deepening this experience with your system by noticing your triggers or what we call **trailheads.** This work will help you see where and how your parts show up in your daily life.

The last phase will walk you through a full IFS healing experience. You will choose one part and work with this part until it is "**unburdened**," bringing more harmony into your mind, body, and life.

This book will walk you through a process of getting to know your parts in a slow, simple way. Once you get to know your parts and your system, we will take a deeper dive into healing the hurting parts of you who may be beneath parts of you that are running your life in a subconscious way that is causing you unhappiness.

This book is about helping you find your protective parts, befriend them and heal what they are protecting so you can live the life you want.

Each chapter as a small step in the journey that leads you to deeper awareness and self- discovery. It is discovery of your parts, and how they are trying to help you and who inside they are trying to protect.

Each step is represented as a word. Each word is a chapter. As you read each word and the chapter, you will have a chance to turn your attention inside to your own mind and body.

This walk is also about reminding you of your True Self. You are not your wall. You are not your perfectionism. You are not your addiction. You are not your anger. You are not your sadness.

You are calm. You are courageous. You are creative. You are reading this, wanting something better for your life.

I am so glad you are here. You are capable of connecting and knowing all of your parts. This book is a slow journey that leads you back to your Self. You are able to be with and hear from all of your younger, hurting parts. You can do this work step by step, day by day, word by word.

DAY 1 · *One*

We are going to spend the next 30 days slowly getting to know the different parts of you, hearing their stories, and creating harmony inside. Every day a new word will guide you deeper into your inner world. Every day will have an opportunity for you to explore your own parts. I hope you carry each daily word with you as you notice and observe yourself. Make you and your inner system the experiment you study.

Mapping your internal system is the process in which you track which part of you is active at a given moment. It is following who inside is driving the bus and understanding what the major parts feel and sound like.

Mapping is paying attention to who is in charge at any given point in a day. You will start noticing patterns and themes. You will start noticing the common parts we all have such as a Critic, an Organizer, a Time Keeper, a Distractor, and a Lover of All the Cookies.

One of the best ways I found to start tracking my parts is having a method or a strategy to help me pay attention to what is happening inside of me. This pauses me from my busy day, from focusing outward and helps me take a You-Turn toward what is happening inside of me.

A few years ago I came across the idea of choosing a single word as a New Year's resolution. I've done it every year since, and encourage my friends, family, and patients to do the same.

My words have been *pause, space, calm,* and *slow.* My word in 2019 was *with* as I want to be fully *with* the people in the moment, not on my phone, not thinking about what is happening next. I want to be *with* whatever part of me is present.

In 2020, my word was *flow,* with my intention being to follow the *flow* I have set and is already moving forward. This helps my distracted parts refocus on what I am doing in the moment and how I want to spend my time for the greater goals I have set. We all had no idea that a pandemic would hit in 2020 and my intention of *flow* would be a perfect help during this uncertain and scary time.

Since I loved the idea of yearlong one-word resolutions, I often will choose a word for a holiday, an upcoming stressful event, or a time when I want to be more intentional and aware. I often have a word come to mind when I am speaking to a friend or a client.

Using one word a day can help you meet your goals since the word is a daily reminder of your intentions. The word is also like a mindfulness bell, reminding you to reconnect to your Self, to nature, and to Spirit.

Meditation is just putting your mind on something intentionally. You may notice parts reacting to the idea of mediation. Pause right now and notice what your body feels like, what goes through your mind. Anything is allowed. Allow any parts who want to speak to you right now to have a voice. You can listen and understand. You do not have to agree or follow. But you can hear.

A gentle reminder: If you can worry, you can meditate. Each word for the next 30 days can be an anchor, a prayer, a returning to who you are meant to be. It is a returning to who you truly are.

The idea of narrowing your focus down to one word is powerful. I am more likely to remember and apply it differently as my day evolves. One word can be carried with me and it can be a goal, a mantra, and an intention. It has helped me to connect greater to a moment, to relationships, to my body, and to my own true Self.

Self is the one inside who we are naturally made to be, the God image inside of us all. It is the higher power, the connection to the universe. Your language may be different, and I encourage you to find and use terms that resonate with your own belief system.

IFS has added to and enhanced my Spiritual life and connection to my belief system, and I know it can do the same for you, no matter what form your Spirituality takes.

You may feel this Self-energy when you watch a sunrise, hike a mountain, walk in nature, or put your toes in the sand. Self is the one observing, listening to the chatter in your head. When you consider your monkey mind, Self is the one considering, the one watching.

Monkey mind is the chatter inside your head telling you ideas and opinions. It is the back and forth and push and pull that creates disharmony inside of us. It is the seesaw inside your mind that can sound like a dialogue, a minor argument, or a full-blown yelling match. It can also be how your mind pays attention to all the details in the room when someone is speaking. Our minds are like monkeys, wildly swinging from one thing to the next.

In addition to Self, we are also made up of parts. Sometimes our parts are young and stuck in the past. They carry our pain, our burdens. We often Exile these away as they hold a lot of upset and emotionally intensity. We also have parts who protect us from feeling these younger vulnerable ones.

We have two kinds of protectors. Managers are proactive; they work hard to make sure we function very well so we don't feel this intensity. They organize and schedule our lives. They are preventive and busy.

Firefighters are reactive, working hard to make sure we survive the fire of big emotions when we are triggered. They are the parts who get us in trouble, who we and our family members do not like very much. One of my firefighters is the part who went looking for a cookie to calm down and quiet the overwhelming feelings.

> **BE NICE** = to keep parents happy
> **EATING FOOD** = feeling safe

One of the most important insights IFS brings us is the idea that parts can carry burdens. Burdens are beliefs, feelings, and memories from the past. A part may believe that she needs to Be Nice in order to be liked. This may have been true for you as a child; the nicer you were, the less chance your parents would yell, hit, ignore, neglect, etc. This part learned an association: nice is safe; it is a way, a strategy to keep you emotionally and physical safe.

It was a wonderful tool, a part needed to help, but you no longer need her to do that. Sometimes, the coping skills we used to help us with stressors and traumas as children are not needed as adults. Or, we have a variety of coping skills as adults that we did not have as children.

Food is a helpful explanation of this. Often, food was a resource we had as children. It helped us when we were sad or confused. We had access to it.

Now, as an adult I have lots of other ways to soothe myself and access to things to help me.

Healing happens when we update our parts and they are connected to Self. Then they can be unburdened from their beliefs so they can be in their natural roles.

We will learn how to do this one day, one word at a time. In the process, you will get to know your parts and your own internal system to bring more harmony into your mind, body, and heart.

For More Connection Today

Grab a journal and write down what you notice from your parts so far. Welcome your numerous parts without judgement, with that soft curiosity that comes from your Self. Let your parts know you want to hear from them and that there is no wrong response. Write what your parts tell you about each word; you'll notice this by reactions you hear in your mind and feelings you experience in your body. You may already be aware of burdens you carry, strategies, and beliefs your parts have used to keep you safe. Write any that come to your mind.

Let's begin with the One inside of you: yourSelf.

DAY 2 · *Self*

Self feels like home. It is that simple.

Home is a metaphor for coming back to your true Self. Home is embodying all 30 words. Home is a shift from thinking in your head to a warmness in your open heart. Home is a stillness that takes over mind and body. Home is found in connecting with your spirituality. Home is found when you are grounded and anchored in this present moment, where you can truly rest and experience flow. These are the promises of Self.

Recall a time and place where you felt this way. Notice what you are experiencing as you revisit that in your memory.

Notice what you feel inside your body. Get as specific as you can. What did you see, smell, and hear? Imagine being there right now and notice what your body feels like as you do.

Self is the term in IFS used to describe the essence of who you really are, your natural state. It is the center, the soul, the spirit one inside of you. It is not affected by trauma, attachment injuries, hurt, and pain. It is not shaped by your life experiences.

Self in IFS is not the same as the ideas around being self-centered, self-ish, self-controlled. When I think about being in Self (or Self-energy as it is sometimes described), I think of times when I am hiking or at the beach. I feel connected to God, centered inside, grounded on this earth. I notice a softness in my face, a slowness in my body, a clearness in my mind. I notice my belly and spine relax, my hands move slower, and my arms feel light.

Self is found in the qualities of C words such as creative, curious, confident, courage, clear minded, and centered. You can assess for Self by making a self inquiry, "How much of one of these C words am I feeling right now?"

Self is the healing agent; it is the source for healing that can take place no matter what your background, your history, your biology. Self is the only resource you need.

Are you wondering why you aren't just in Self all the time? Me too! But we are not, and that is not our goal. When I started this journey, I thought I would be floating around like a monk who meditates all day long. But, no.

Your Self gets covered up over and over by parts throughout your life in order to protect you. Parts who needed to help you deal with various hurts and pains came online and at the expense of Self, who started to recede deeper inside.

Parts begin to feel more distant from Self, and you feel like you actually are the parts who protect you rather than the Self you truly are. For example, you may feel like you are the critic who tells you that you are bad. Or, you may feel like the perfectionist who keeps you anxious. Or, you may feel like you are your depression.

This is the first big mental shift that happens. Those are parts of you, not all of you, and certainly not who you are.

This part can feel like disharmony and disconnection inside. It can feel like turmoil and conflict. Internal harmony happens when my parts feel like they have an open line of communication with Me, when they feel like my Self is here and listening. One of my first experiences with IFS was with working with a 10-year-old part who was grieving the loss of the relationship I had with my mom when she married my stepdad. As I met this part and sat with her as she was sobbing, I heard her say to me, "You are finally here."

I could see in my imagination this little girl who was crying, and I (Self) sat with her. I felt calm and love for her. I did not feel afraid of what she was feeling or what it meant.

We describe this as "Self being with a part." I am not flooded or overwhelmed. I am experiencing compassion and warmth toward her and in my body.

Your parts want to feel you, they want you to show up and be with them. It's important to know: Self is accessible to you at all times. Your parts are waiting for leadership, for an adult with resources to help them and be with them in the ways they need.

I like to think of Self like the Sun.

I saw the sunrise this morning over the ocean but it didn't rise out of the ocean, it rose out of the clouds laying on top. I could tell the sun was up because of the brightness of the sky although I couldn't see the sun itself. Ten minutes later it suddenly made its appearance, rising up out of the clouds.

The sun is there, even through the clouds.

Parts of you can be critical and mean. They may tell you that you are stupid and no good. They call you names and tell you that you are not worthy or lovable. They lead you to believe you don't deserve kindness, goodness or faithfulness. They may tell you that you deserve the bad things are happening and are not deserving of good things.

These are like the clouds.

Parts of you feel anxious and overwhelmed. You have an ongoing list of all the things which are wrong with you that you need to change. Another part yells that you have too much to do stating, "When are you going to get it all done?!"

More clouds.

Parts hold pain in your body: headaches, stomachaches, backaches. A part tells you, "You will always feel this way. You are no good. This proves it. You are broken. Nobody will ever want you."

Clouds.

Parts can be overcome by past memories, hurts, pain, and abuse. They tell you beliefs about yourself and show you images and sounds and smells that you cannot forget.

So cloudy, so dark.

Parts want to shop, to spend, to eat, to drink, to watch, to look, to distract, to numb. "It is too hard. I have to do this. I can't stop."

On a cloudy day, it looks like there is no sun. On a cloudy day, it seems like there will not be a sunrise. On a cloudy day, it feels like there is no sun at all.

The sun is always there beneath the clouds. The sun is the God light in us. It is our natural birthright. It is who we were made to be. Before the burdens, before the pain, before the hurt.

It is an anchor in the midst of rough seas. It is the sun inside of us all; in our minds and our hearts and our bodies.

Self is inside of us still although we can't see it behind the clouds.

Self *is* the coping skill.

Often I receive a new patient email which says a person wants to come to therapy because they want coping skills. Parents want their kids to have coping skills. "Little David throws a temper when things don't go his way, so he needs coping skills."

Or, "When my boss calls me into his office, I begin to have a nervous breakdown so I need coping skills."

Or, "My wife cries (or my husband yells) when I do such and such so I need coping skills to deal with them."

I get it. I want a fix, too. I feel something BAD and I need to FIX it with a coping skill. I need a tool, to fix the BAD with a tool.

My internal response to this could sound like: "You need to give them a list of the 10 best coping skills from USA Today. And quickly. Otherwise, they will think you are a failure. And will tell everyone in the world. You will never have a new patient. The ones you do have will quit. You will have to close your practice and stay home, sit on the couch, and eat bon bons."

Whoa. Now I have some pretty intense reactions to this because a part believes if I don't give them coping skills I will lose my livelihood, my career, my purpose, my identity! My Lose It All part carries some big feelings with it.

Self looks at Lose It All and smiles. "Hi. Are you feeling a bit dramatic?"

"Why, yes, Yes I am. Thanks for noticing."

Self and this part have a laugh together.

Self puts her arm around this sweet part and lets her know that I get she is trying to help us be a good therapist because we want to be helpful.

This part feels understood and calmer in Self's embrace.

I immediately feel more relaxed. My heart has slowed down and I am not feeling the pressure and urgency I was before I connected with this part.

This is called **"unblending."** Self has to unblend enough from a part to see it, to hear it, to experience it as separate from it. I am a Self and have a part. We will return to this idea again and again.

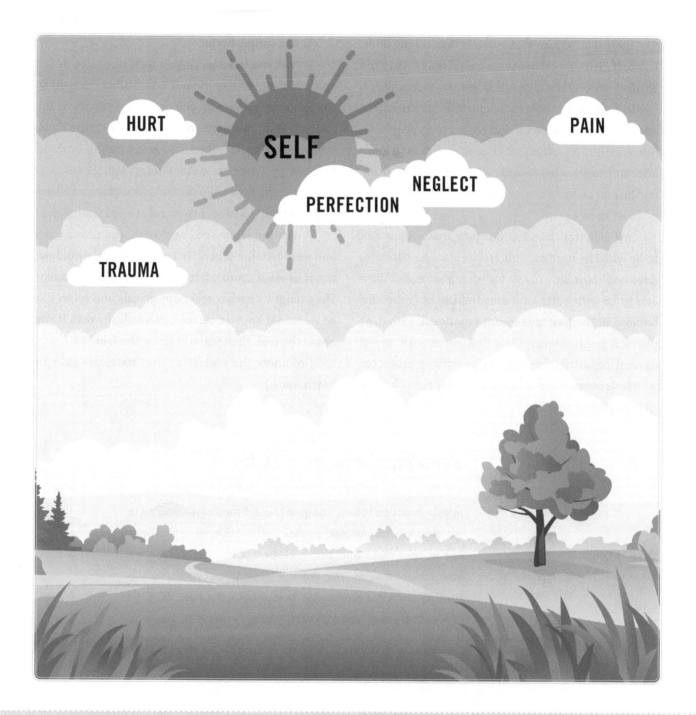

There is an answer that is better than coping skills. It is Self. Self calmed down my parts' reactions to the emails I wrote about above. Self was the coping skill.

In Self, I know how to handle difficult situations, overwhelming emotions, and challenging people. In Self, I feel into situations, so I know when to set boundaries and limits, what relationships to walk away from, and how to be more attuned to my body's responses.

Self knows.

Self is better than 1,000 coping tools. Allow Self to be with the hurting, vulnerable, younger part who does not know how to ask for what she needs. Allow Self to be with parts who are afraid to be "called in" because in the past this meant emotional, verbal, or physical punishment. Allow Self to be with angry, overeating/drinking/shopping, avoidant protector who feels overwhelmed and needs a way out of having to feel in order to survive.

Self is simply better.

I want you to know what it feels like to be in Self and what it feels like in your body. Where do you go to reconnect, relax? Can you imagine going there and imagine the sensations in your body? Breathe down into your belly and feel your body expanding. Feel this Self-energy (warmth, calm, energy, light, or waves) flowing from your belly down to your toes and back all the way up to your throat and around your mind.

A very long time ago I worked at a bank as a teller and went to teller school. In teller school, they did not teach us what counterfeit money feels and looks like. They taught us what real money feels and looks like so we would know what was authentically real. If you know the real, then you will know the fake.

So, know the real. (Not that parts are fake by any means.)

For More Connection Today

 In your practice today, imagine those times when you were feeling more connected to your Self. Notice what this feels like in your mind and body. Notice your posture. Notice your facial muscles. You will continue to get to know this true you, this Authentic Self throughout the next 30 days and well beyond. You will be reminded of who you are meant to be, who you truly are.

DAY 3 *Parts*

We are all multiple; it is the natural state of our minds. We all have "mini minds" or sub-personalities who have different gifts, abilities, and roles. Our internal system includes parts who protect called Managers and Firefighters, parts who need protecting called Exiles, and a center called Self.

Managers work hard to ensure the exiled feelings are never felt. They plan, schedule, and strategize so you never feel the shame, badness, despair, panic, and fear of the exiles. Firefighters work hard after an exile's feelings are triggered. They soothe with alcohol, anger, food, gambling, pornography, and dissociation. The main difference between these protective parts is their order; one keeps the exile energy from taking over, and one tries to stop it once it does.

The part of me who rides the roller coaster is different than the one who does my taxes. The part who eats all the things when my husband is late getting home from work is different than the part of me who has a glass of wine before dinner with my in-laws.

The roller coaster may be a younger teenage part who just wants to have fun! The inner accountant feels very serious and quite annoyed with my spending habits. Both of these parts feel different in my body.

The worried part uses food to calm down when son is late arriving home from school. Another part anticipates feeling uncomfortable uses wine to help settle down. One is a firefighter: the upset is happening, and it is trying to help immediately to calm down the upset. One is a manager: the upset may happen in the future, and it is trying to think ahead to keep the upset at bay.

Notice the reactions you hear inside of you as you read these ideas. You may already start noticing similar parts inside. You may be experiencing parts that sound like your own voice in your mind. Maybe you notice a reaction in your body. You may lean back, your heart may race a bit more, or your hands may shake or become warm.

Begin to think of these as parts of you. A part thinks you know this already, another part is skeptical, and a part thinks you need to put this down and do the laundry. All parts are valid and their concerns are welcome.

A part of me will eat an entire box of cookies and another part will choose the Wendy's salad, which has

20 calories less than other salads. On the same day. True story.

I have a part who Eats All the Cookies because this is a way of soothing she learned to do when she was young. I have another part who is Embarrassed by her and does not want me to share that with you. A different part is Critical of both, stating the cookie eater is lazy and embarrassment is ridiculous. Those three parts can go around and around creating disharmony.

Despite what you may be feeling and thinking right now, all parts are valuable and have good intentions. My Cookie Eater part is trying to soothe me, my Embarrassed part wants to make sure I am accepted, and my Critical part is trying to protect me from others' criticism.

All parts are trying to help and protect. They have a limited view and limited knowledge of their experience because they are stuck in the past. The way they learned how to protect is the only way they believe will work to protect.

Parts heal with connection to Self. Remember, Self is the tool, the healing agent.

The Cookie Eater, Embarrassed one, and Critic create a lot of tension in my mind and body. Self shows up and says, "Hi. I see how hard you all are working. I see you all. I want to talk to you all one at a time." Self comes into the room and tension and chatter stops immediately. Instead of all looking at one another, they look at Self, who is curious about each of their jobs and roles. They feel that attention and curiosity. They can speak and know their voice and opinions are valued. I feel my whole body settle.

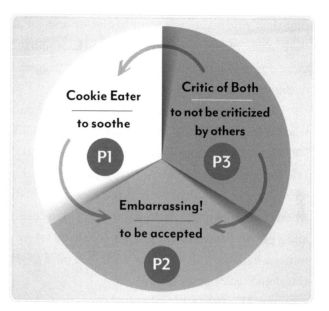

Let's say you notice a critical part telling you that you are just a no-good, awful, horrible person. Another part feels angry toward this part. Now you have two parts: a Critical one, and an Angry one. If you want to get to know the Critic then you need to ask Anger to give you some room so you, in Self, can get to know the Critic in order to heal. The Critic is your focus, your target part.

We will talk about asking parts for space later, but try this first. You will be surprised at the result.

Anger gives you space so Self can connect to Critic. Then, you learn that Critic is just trying to make sure you never fail. The Critic actually wants to protect us from failure, and it is good at its job. The fact that the Critic makes you feel ashamed and not good enough doesn't matter to the critic. Even the fact that the Critic makes you want to give up and eat all the cookies, making you gain weight and hate yourself more doesn't matter to it either. (The critic triggers a firefighter, which we will talk about later.)

Here's an example from Day Two with the part who said to me, "If you don't give clients coping skills, you will end up sitting on the couch eating bon bons." I close my eyes and check in with this part by recalling what the client said and what it felt like in my body when that happened. I notice a fluttering in my heart and a pitching forward like action needs to be taken. I notice a narrowing of my vision and, "You need to get this done!" voice in my head.

I say "Hi" with an open-hearted curiosity and wait until she can notice me. I see an image of a Pacing Girl; she looks to be about 13 years old. She is very stressed and overwhelmed. She begins to tell me her worries and fears. She worries we will lose our identity and we will become the person we always feared we were: lazy and unproductive.

I let her know that I hear her and welcome the fears and beliefs she holds. I let her know I see how hard she works to make sure that fear never comes true. I let her know that I am here. I can take care of her. She is only 13 years old and is carrying a lot of pressure and expectations. I can feel her relax a bit. As I feel connected to her, my body softens even more.

My Pacing Girl part, as is true for all parts, got forced into roles through childhood experiences, injuries, and trauma. Younger parts can get frozen in time, locked away, and exiled. Protective parts end up in roles they believe will keep us safe and will keep us from feeling flooded by the vulnerable feelings of the young, exiled parts.

This part (a manager) is protecting a younger part (an exile) who feels not good enough and feels like she has to perform in order to be loved. So, my 13-year-old is a performing queen. And, she is very good at her job.

For More Connection Today

 Start to map out your parts. You can do this by noticing when you are having a strong feeling, reaction, or engaging in an unwanted behavior. Your thoughts, your facial expressions, your behaviors, your feelings, your bodily sensations all give you a clue.

Write it down. You will have similar parts pop up every day. Begin to notice themes and your major players or "go-to" parts and how they show up.

Begin this new way of thinking. A part of me tells me _____. I know a part of me is present by my racing heart, upset stomach, tense shoulders, etc. A part wanted cookies, while another part feels guilty for eating them.

Take your time. This is new and there is no rush. All you are doing is noticing and mapping. What you are doing is getting a bit more clarity about your parts and how they sound and feel.

DAY 4 · Space

Hopefully, you are starting to get a good sense of your Self and beginning to map your parts as you connect with them. You want to get to know parts by having more Self-energy with them. One important question to help tease this out is to ask, "What am I feeling toward this part?"

Let's say I wanted to get to know someone named Ms. Critical so I took her out to coffee. Another friend came who does not like Ms. Critical. Is Ms. Critical going to open up about her hurts and feelings with Dislike rolling her eyes every time she spoke? Probably not.

If I want to get to know a part, I need to have an open heart and possibly some curiosity or another C-word quality such as compassion, clarity, or clear-mindedness.

When trying to get to know one part, you can ask how am I feeling toward it? If you sense anything other than a C-word quality or even more neutrality, you want to ask for space from this other part. You will likely have parts who do not like the target part you are trying to get to know.

If you feel discomfort, dislike, anger, etc. then you do not have enough Self energy to really connect to the target part. If you are feeling angry, frustrated, irritated, or defensive then you are in a part and want

to ask for space. If you are feeling argumentative or if you feel like you are that part, you want to ask for space so you, as Self can connect to the original part.

Keep asking for space until you notice a C-word like quality or even a neutral feeling. You can ask parts to go into a waiting room, to step back, to even go do something else. They may not want to be involved in the conversation and you can let them know they do not have to be and give them permission to be dismissed. If parts keep interfering with your target part, you may need to spend more time with them and find out what they want you to know or what they are afraid would happen if you did connect more with the target part.

I need to ask Dislike to wait outside the coffee shop so I can have space to get to know Ms. Critical. I hear from Ms. Critical that she tells me mean things about myself in order to protect me from trying and failing. She would rather see me not try at all then feel like a failure or to actually fail. She says this is the worst feeling and she does what she needs to do in order to keep me from this experience. Now, I have more information about why this part says things to me and how she is trying to help.

Showing parts appreciation and compassion for the hard work they do to keep us safe and opens up space for more Self-energy. Letting the part know you see their positive intentions helps it communicate.

We each need two types of space: 1) is space from other parts who do not like or want us close to our "target part"; and 2) is space from the target part itself in order to get to know it.

An example of Internal Space:

I have a part who yells, "Get it right!" when I begin asking IFS-like questions with patients. This part says to me, "You don't know what you are doing!" I have other parts who feel panicked by this who try to appease it by changing questions and other parts who get mad by its criticism.

I ask this group of parts to give space so I can give more curiosity to the "get it right" part with an open heart. I assure them that their reaction makes sense and if they let me meet with this part, I will be able to help it. They agree to do this.

The Get It Right part feels male and told me he doesn't want anything to do with therapy *at all*. (I picture him with balled fists down by his sides.) He would rather play on the floor with cars. I ask him how old he is. My clue is his balled fists and car play, and he tells

me he is six. I let him know that he doesn't have to do therapy, I will (Self). He can play with cars. So, he is doing just that. I may want to ask further questions to find out why he is there and what are his needs.

Now, I am not sure why he feels like he needed to help in the therapy room. I'm not sure why my system pushed him forward. I could ask him and I could ask the system and see what they say. For now, this feels complete. When I begin to have similar feelings in session in the future, I picture that little boy and remind him that he can play with cars.

This connection to him would not have happened if the group reacting to this voice stayed active.

Space allows for connection to one part, to be able to see it more clearly and build a friendship with it. Space also allows for more Self to be with the part. In this case, space allows for Self to do therapy, not a confused younger part of me.

Think of space as room inside of you where you experience expansion and lightness. Space to breathe. Space to be your Self. Space for your parts to be with you. Space also helps us isolate the target part so we do not feel like we *are* them, but we are *with* them.

For More Connection Today

As you begin to focus on more of your go-to parts, notice how you feel toward each one. If it is not a C-like word, you may be in another part. Ask parts to give you space to deepen your friendship and connection with the target part so you can get to know it. Notice how this spaciousness allows for more Self to flow through you.

DAY 5 Connection

If you and I were trying to get to know each other we would need some sort of connection. This is also true with our parts. We need to connect to parts and have them feel us connecting in order to meet them, befriend them, and heal the burdens they carry.

One way we connect to parts is by "going inside" with eyes shut or cast down in order to focus, whichever feels safe. This is not necessary, but it is helpful. By shutting my eyes I am better able to focus on my inward experience. I am better able to notice sensations in my body, thoughts in my mind, or images of my parts.

Some people do not see images of their parts and some do. I am very visual so seeing my parts in one of the ways I connect with them and begin having a relationship with them. You can do the same thing with connecting to a bodily sensation or a belief.

It is helpful to connect with one part, to highlight a part, as a way to localize it or to feature it. You want to hear, to sense, to feel what it is like when this part drives the bus or conducts the orchestra or facilitates the meeting. I suggest picking one metaphor that works for you where you sense or picture where your parts gather. I like to use the image of a big house, a mansion with a giant dining room table where we can all gather.

You can go inside and ask, "Who is up? Who is here? Who is driving the bus? Who is gathered around the table? Who wants my attention?" For example, I can invite all my parts around a table who have something to say about eating.

When you are triggered by something, you can imagine asking all parts involved to come to the table. You can look around the table and ask each part what they want you to know so they all have a voice with you.

Parts speak to us in our mind and body. I know I am in a part by the words I hear in my head and the tension I feel in my body. The first thing I want to do is connect with this part by focusing my attention on it. Just like getting to know what Self feels like, it is helpful to know what you typically experience when you are in a part. It is important information so you can connect to the part and listen in to what it wants to say. It is also important to let the parts know you are not trying to get rid of them but actually you

are leaning into them so you can get to know them more fully.

One of my go to parts is my Clipboard Manager. I know she is running the show, driving the bus, or at the head of the table when I move and talk fast. I may be physically shaking with a long list in my head, and I don't make eye contact with others. I am in doing mode. I am very familiar with this feeling and as I connect with her, I know she is an important part in my system as she tends to run my life. I hear inside, "You need me to run your life. Otherwise, you would be on the couch eating bon bons."

Apparently, several of my other parts also have this same concern.

Connecting parts to Self will look different for everyone. For me, connecting to my body helps me first begin to notice what parts are activated. Taking a few deep breaths, I bring my attention to my body. This relaxes my parts who can be busy, over thinking, and hyper. It helps me slow down and connect to my body and to this moment.

I imagine sinking down into my body as I notice my breath come into my belly, my heart, and my nose helping me feel more embodied. I am now open and ready to hear from the part I want to get to know and befriend. I am ready to connect.

For More Connection Today

 Where do you notice the movement of your breath? Nose, chest, or stomach? Follow this as you sink into your body and give your mind (a thinking part) a rest. Can you connect deeper to this moment as you sink in to your body? As you sink in, let your parts know you are curious and interested in getting to know each of them. Ask for space from the parts of you who want to get rid of them or judge them.

Do they notice you desiring to connect? What is that like for them? Do you visualize them and if so, does it make sense to have them come into a room, a table, a house, or a garden? It is okay if none of these fit for your system. Try out a few and choose one that makes sense.

DAY 6 Curious

I believe in the power of words. One word can change your life and this was the one that did it for me. This is the word that did it for me when I was at the dreadful conference in which I was nothing more than bored. The only reason I was at the conference was because it was an excuse to hang out with a therapist friend that I only saw as we passed each other in the hallway getting our clients from the waiting room.

I hate basketball yet I joined a team in middle school because all my friends did. Then they quit but my mom wouldn't let me because we had already paid the fee. I was the only one on the team who never, ever scored a basket. I don't have any parts about that. Obviously.

Curiosity is still my favorite C word.

I am curious about the part of me who agreed to go to a child therapy training when I do not see children in my practice and to play a sport I don't like just because my friends did. What I first notice is annoyance. I feel that in my body as tension in my chest and I experience it in my mind as a thought, "You are so lame."

I invite all the parts of me who have anything to do with this topic around a table. I am at the front of the table, looking out at them all. I don't see anything particularly but I hear opinions. I let them know I am curious about why they are there and what they want to say. I hear a Critical part of the others, a part who does not want to Miss Out on fun things with friends, a part who is Afraid of being alone. I smile and thank them all for being there. I feel calmer and I no longer feel that tension or criticism.

Imagine if you were curious about a behavior you did that you wish you did not do. Or, you were curious about a behavior you wanted to do but didn't. I wonder what you would experience if you ask the parts who are thinking and analyzing your behavior to step back and ask for curiosity to step forward. Notice how different that feels inside.

What is it like for you to be curious about a feeling you are experiencing instead of immediately trying to push it away? I wonder how it would be for you if you leaned into a feeling with curiosity, interest, and attention.

I'm curious about the parts who continue to engage in unhealthy behaviors. I'm curious about my emotional reaction (a part) to someone difficult in my life. I'm curious about an exaggerated response (again, a part) to an event or a person.

Remember what it was like when I brought Self (curiosity) to my critical parts in the past few days? If I felt overwhelming shame from these critical parts, I may have numbed out with TV or sugar until the feeling went away never learning about who inside me felt this way and why. I would have actually just reinforced this part's strategy of helping.

Curiosity helps your intellectualizing and analytical parts step back (give space) and softens the parts of you who feel a lot of shame. Connecting to your parts with curiosity helps strengthen and isolate the target part.

For More Connection Today

 Curiosity is a quality of Self; it is a sign you are experiencing Self energy. When you do something you later regret or wish you didn't do, bring curiosity in by closing your eyes, saying "Hello" to the part who did that, and regarding it with curiosity. See what comes up and see if that part will be more open about how it is trying to help you. Try experimenting with bringing parts around a table and sending them all curiosity.

DAY 7 *Unblend*

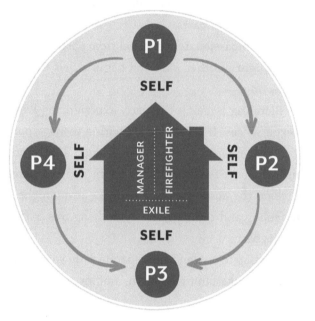

Unblending is the term that means separating out Self from a part so the part is not taking over the system. The part can be a helper, an advisor, or a copilot, but we want the Self in the driver's seat, in the lead. I can get wisdom and information from the part, but I am led by the Self. We are not trying to get rid of parts, we want to befriend them and heal them so they are no longer stuck in roles they find exhausting.

My son is trying to talk to me, but I am distracted by a manager part who is Moving Fast and trying to get things done like cook, laundry, dishes, etc. Hopefully, I turn my head, my attention, my focus from these activities to my son. I focus on him by moving my attention away from these other things. They are still there, and I will tend to them soon. I unhook my attention from these tasks, turning my focus from the activity to him.

We do this when we go inside, too. We turn our attention from the outside of us in our environment and world to what is happening on the inside of us in our minds and bodies.

Another way to explain unblending is to consider a spotlight on a stage. I want whatever part I am curious about, my target part to be in the spotlight. I will not be able to get to know a Fearful part who is afraid I'm going to get in trouble when my boss calls me into the office if I am only focused on the Critical part calling me weak and a big baby. If I ask the Critical part to give me a little room, space on the stage so I can put the Fearful one in the spotlight, it may do that. I let it know I hear its concerns. I may negotiate with it by addressing its fears and maybe it just stands outside of the light. Now the one I want to turn attention to is in the spotlight.

We subtract parts by asking them to give space, and then they unblend from us and each other. As we separate parts by asking for space, Self emerges. We are not trying to get rid of parts, and parts do not become integrated into the Self. We ask for separation, an unblending of parts.

We compassionately unblend from parts in order to highlight another part and begin a Self to part connection.

Blending is being the part, experiencing what it experiences. If I am blended with a teenage part I may feel enraged as I yell at my friend, "That is not fair!" when she tells me I should not buy an expensive purse on the home shopping network at midnight. I am feeling and thinking and embodying this part. I am this part.

Starting to unblend and separate from your parts could look like taking a breath, smiling, and saying "Hello" to the part as you feel a strong reaction that may not fit with the circumstances or feel like it is coming from my adult Self. As I practice this smiling and saying "Hello," I feel the part separate from me, giving me space from it so I can experience it more clearly. I picture the part and hear what it has to say. I let it know I hear it.

One way to unblend is to intentionally blend with a part. It is like asking the part to use your hand, mind, or body to express its needs to you. I like doing this in my journal where I let my parts say whatever they want. They can control the pen. When I let them say what they want in an exaggerated, intentional way, I smile and feel love for her. I am blended with her, and I am aware that she is not me, she is with me and I am with her. We are connected.

This is a powerful practice. I write a P, for part, and let the part say whatever it wants. I write P2 for other parts who react to the first, P3 for the next part and so on. I write S for Self who says to all of them, "I am here, I am listening."

For More Connection Today

 Play with several of these methods to use in order to focus, highlight, and feature a part by unblending from it. Notice what this experience is like for your system. Try writing from one of your parts. What does it want to say as you lean into it? Let it know that it can use your hand to write whatever it wants to write. Note other parts' reactions to it. You can even try writing in different colors or writing in your nondominant hands. Then, say "Hello" from Self. Write out what your heart, your adult Self wants to say to them. Let them all know you are right there.

DAY 8 | *Polarized*

Most people are familiar with the devil and angel on the shoulder idea. Let's rethink this using what you know about parts and your system so far. The part on one side says, "Go outside and cut the grass," while the part on the other side says, "Stay inside and watch TV." And you, as the part in the middle, have to decide which to listen to.

We do not choose a part or label any as good/right or bad/wrong. We understand both have good intentions. Both want our attention, and both are often protecting the same vulnerable exile.

If I just picked one and isolated the other, I would miss this. And there may be some backlash from the other part.

If I just listened to the Cut Grass part, I may end up feeling more tired and resentful. I may hear, "I never get a chance to rest! I am always doing stuff." Then I may call out of work the next day. If I just listened to the Stay Inside and Watch TV, I may feel overwhelmed by all the chores I need to do and I may hear, "You cannot keep up with your responsibilities." Then I may call out of work the next day.

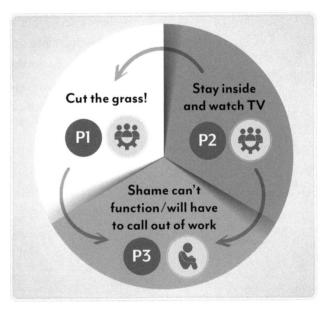

If I listen to both equally with curiosity, I hear they both want the best for me. They want me to do the things I need to do, and they want me to rest and take care of myself. I ask them both what they are afraid would happen if I did not listen to them. They both say they do not want me to feel ashamed and believe my life is unmanageable. Previously, they were angry with each other but now they understand they are on the same team. I thank them both and we agree that we will cut the grass and then relax and watch TV. We have time for both.

Then, we will not call out and feel the shame of the belief, "You can't manage your life."

The "family" idea of IFS is just this, we have parts who interact with each other, parts who align together, and parts who go head-to-head against one another. Parts don't just interact with us; they interact with one another.

Sometimes parts do not want to do a thing because of another parts' influence. This is referred to as polarization, the idea that two parts are opposing or in conflict and impacting each other.

Here's another example. I woke up today feeling tired and overwhelmed. I did not want to get out of bed. I looked inside and noticed a younger part who wanted to Stay in Bed all day. I let her know that she could stay in bed, and I (the Self) would go to work. She seemed frightened by something at the door. When I brought my attention that, I noticed a Pacing part that was ready to hit me with a huge to do list.

Of course, she wanted to stay in bed; she was scared of the pacing part. I soothed the pacing part by asking it to sit, to write down what I needed to remember. I assured it that I would listen later once I was up and around. This calmed *both* parts down because they had my attention and were not so aroused by each other.

I can see how one part wants me to be productive and one part wants me to rest. Both have my best interests at heart. Both know these are important values to me. Both are protecting me from the more intense feelings of a vulnerable, younger part of me who feels like she is not good enough. Often two parts who are polarized like this are trying to protect me from the same exile.

When I inquire with curiosity and an open heart, I see a 12-year-old girl laying on the couch feeling melancholy. I hear her say she needs to do this to put up with all the family stress. When I was 12 years old, I had a 2-year-old half-sister, my 13-year-old stepsister is causing my mom a lot of stress, and I go to my dad's every other weekend. I understand and I hear how much stress this little girl had going on and see she needed a break. I let her know I get this.

I turn my attention to the one who is Pacing. She says, "Don't waste the day!" and I see the same scene where my 12-year-old is being "a lazy bones" on the couch, and my mom is vacuuming. This part wants to please mom, wants to help mom be less stressed, and says we can do that by getting up and being a helpful, good girl.

I smile at both and let them know I see how they are both in the same memory, the same scene of my childhood. I wonder what they are protecting and I get a deep feeling of sadness in my eyes and chest. This is the part who feels she Lost Her Mom when she married my stepdad. I let them know I see how they both work hard to keep me up and out of this dark, intense experience.

Often parts are stuck in the past and do not know we are no longer in that same situation. My 12-year-old part does not know we no longer live with that amount of tension and chaos. The Stay in Bed part and the Huge to do List part try to protect me from feelings of her. Stay in bed away from all the chaos or try to keep ahead of the chaos with the to do list.

Parts have fixed roles based on the past and how our systems needed them in our history. You could call them defense mechanisms, as they are a way your parts learned how to deal with something in the past (like dissociation during trauma). These parts' strategies or defense mechanisms are no longer needed as the initial situation is no longer occurring. This could be trauma, neglect, or just the typical stresses of growing up.

Healing comes when parts are transformed to have different roles now that their strategies are no longer necessary. We do not get rid of parts; we help them unburden so they can fulfill their natural role in our system.

Defense mechanisms are parts; they are ways parts learned to cope.

Parts are often inflexible. I don't need my "lazy bones" or the 'Don't waste the day!' parts to go away, but I need them to be flexible and make a compromise. Self knows we can do both, and there is plenty of time in the day. Updating the 12-year-old is the first step in releasing the protector parts (sleep all day and to do list) of their roles. When Self is connected to the 12-year-old (the Exile), the protective parts do not have to work as hard. They can actually begin to imagine doing another job.

Polarized parts are not flexible; they actually have to be more extreme in their positions so they can make their point. They only look at the part who is opposite. It is like a tug of war. They do not see you or know you. They may believe the "you" is the other part.

It is as if the angel and devil keeping looking back and forth at each other. They do not see you and are desperate to make their point.

Parts are not aware of how their roles effect other parts of us. Sometimes parts have an idea of the best way to handle a situation or take care of us. They think their idea is the only one that works. They wave their hand high in the air as if to say, "I know the solution!" without thinking or caring about the consequences.

My Eat All the Chocolate part knows without a shadow of doubt chocolate will help me feel better right now and it is not flexible until it meets Self. Self can say, "Hi, I see you and appreciate you. There may be another way to soothe us." Eat All the Chocolate is polarized with a part who wants to be healthier. The tug of war they can play is relentless until they meet Self and learn a new way.

For More Connection Today

 Notice your major players who are polarized. You may find them in your black-and-white, all-or-nothing thought patterns. Unblend from both remembering you are not either of them, you are in the middle. Ask for Space and, with curiosity, listen to their concerns and intentions for you. They both want to help you and both are working hard to protect a younger part. Bring curiosity to both and check to see if you feel the same way toward both of them. Ask for space from parts until you do. Then let them know how you feel and ask them what they are afraid would happen if they did not do what they do. This will give you a hint into what they are protecting.

DAY 9 · *Embodied*

Parts and Self show up in our bodies. This may be with tension or pain. It may be with a rigid posture or with becoming smaller and closed in. We can use our bodies to identify parts and to unblend. We can invite our bodies to show us what having more Self energy feels.

One of my first tells or cues that I am blended with a thinking part is that I feel tension in my face, which has contributed to deepening a wrinkle in the middle of my brow. Another part suggests Botox.

This tension in my face has become a reminder that I am in a part. I use this cue as an invitation to move my energy from my thinking mind down my body into my center. It is one of my markers; a marker I am in a part.

When I notice this, I shift from the intellectualizing, Figure-It-Out part to a more heart opening. I imagine breathing in and out through my heart. This can feel like energy moving from my head into the center of my being, my heart. For others, it may feel like the energy moves to your gut center. Try both and see which one feels more like home in your body.

Sometimes just a smile and three deep breaths can create this shift. As you soften my body, you soften your parts allowing for more space for Self.

Another marker I am in a part is how much I move. I am mover. I move my hands as I talk. My mind moves fast. I move my body, sometimes in a complete circle as I am doing 10 things at once. I say Hi to my Clipboard Manager part. I adore her and she helps me get a lot done.

Taking a pause can make a difference in how I am experiencing each event in my body. I let my managerial, busy parts know I will still be productive and efficient (some of their fears). I can still move, and I can take a moment to pause in between things. I feel like I don't rush throughout the day, and I am not as exhausted by the end.

I really need to work with my part who, once I am up and moving in the morning, can bombard me with ideas because they do not trust I will get it all done. They know I am full busy or full stop, a common polarization in my system. I'm not actually sure it is true that I go full stop or full go but it is what some

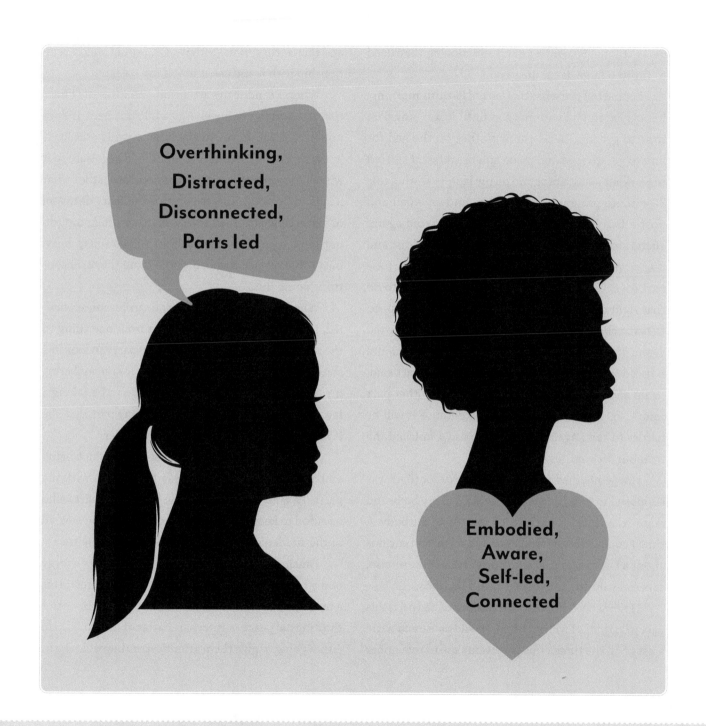

parts tell me. So, while I'm up and moving they need to throw a huge list at me.

Let me tell you what this looked like this morning: I snuggled in bed with my son until it was way past time to get up. Then I threw clothes on the bed for him to get dressed and made him breakfast. I started to workout using a program on my laptop. During this 30-minute program, I stopped to find an email and post a handout on Facebook. Then I started again. Then I stopped to look up numbers of the podcast and text someone who asked me about it yesterday (one part says, "Oh you forgot to do that, you need to do that right now.") Then I started again. Then I stopped to text a client about a schedule change. Then I started again. Then I noticed I was incredibly distracted and noticed irritation and annoyance. Another part said, "Stop and attend to these details!" And another part said, "No, you'll regret that all day because it will be harder to start again." Needless to say, I finished the workout 45 minutes later.

How embodied was I doing my workout!? It was supposed to be a time when I could feel my body and enjoy it. A time I could have connected to my body. A time I could have enjoyed more fully. I'm also curious about a Distracted part who presents during exercise, especially during the more difficult sections.

I know I need to work with this Distracted part, this part who thinks I will not listen. I could pause and write a list of all the things this part wants me to remember and then return to my activity. Or, I could build a relationship with it and ask it to remind me later.

When I send it my attention and interest, I hear that it needs to use my energy while it is here, it does not trust I will have energy later. I smile and let it know that it isn't wrong. We are able to negotiate so it will let me write a list down and decide together what needs to be done. This is some of the fears of my all or nothing parts. They worry that I am full stop (do not want to get off the couch) or full go (busy, busy, busy). The deeper this belief, the more they will continue doing this.

When I work with my parts and can be more embodied, I glide instead of rush. I glide from one thing to the next. Pausing to be with my Busy part can look like stating an intention, reading a passage, or remembering my word for the day or year. Pausing can be taking a few deep breaths. It is a reminder to my part that she is important and I will spend time with her.

Because my parts equate rushing with not being embodied, pausing is good way to check in with my parts. Pausing can also help me connect to parts who use food to keep me out of my body (Have you ever all of the sudden eaten 1,000 cookies? No, me neither.)

Pausing is a way to connect to more Self-energy in my body, allowing my parts to soften and rest. It is a break to help shift from the external noise to notice the internal peace or internal chatter of my parts. I am either going to give them attention or they will take it.

For More Connection Today

 What does being embodied feel like for you? What helps you feel more embodied? Notice what parts do not want you to be in your body. Practice breathing in and out of your heart. Practice breathing in and out of your gut.

Bring curiosity to your busy bee parts. What do they sound like and feel like? Pause during times of distraction and bring curiosity to your distracted parts. Distraction is a great way a part may keep you from being embodied. There are many understandable reasons your parts may not want you connected to your body. Listen, pause, and show compassion. Let them know you want to hear their concerns. Try using your word from each day as a reminder to connect to your body in the moment.

DAY 10 *Clarity*

I'm on my paddleboard and I turn a corner into the wind heading back home. I hear parts arguing inside my mind:

PART ONE: "You should not have gone this far!" I feel my heart racing.

PART TWO: "Will you just shut up! You are ruining this experience. Just look up and keep going."

PART THREE: "Why do you always do this? What is wrong with you? You need to think about why you keep making these stupid mistakes."

I immediately notice a Thinking part in my head. I notice this by tension on the sides of my face, like my head is in a vice grip. I am focusing on the "whys." Why did I keep going? Why didn't I turn around?

I step back from these parts and look at them with compassion, knowing they have my best interests at heart. I am not identified by one, they are all parts of me, and I am slightly removed from them. I let them

know I hear them. I continue to notice my Why part, so I turn my attention to this part. I am blended and can only hear "Why!?" and feel tension around my brows.

I let this part know I want to hear from it but cannot do it when it is too close. I ask it to move slightly away from me so I can see it more clearly. It agrees and I see a big head on a little body. I smile at it and say "Hello." I ask it what he wants me to know.

The Why tells me that if it helps me figure this out, I will never do this again. It wants to help me analyze myself and think about what I do and why I do it. It also keeps me from feeling in my body; it keeps me in my mind away from big feelings.

I feel more clear-minded. I look up from my paddleboard and see what is around me. I'm more aware of what my senses are taking in. I look up and paddle home.

Parts do not have the clarity of Self. The parts who intellectualize, analyze, and ask "Why?" do not have Self's full perspective. Being with these parts and listening to them fosters trust. Self has clarity that the parts do not have. Self is in the present and parts are often stuck in the past. Parts have their own specific agenda, but the Self's agenda is for healing and reconciliation of the system.

You can let your parts know they do not have all the information you do; they do not have the whole scene. They often do not know how old you are and what inner strength, ideas, and external supportive resources you have now.

You, in Self, have the clarity your system desires. When stressed, with a spinning, active mind, we are often hyper-focused on one thing or one thought. Instead of fighting to figure out an answer to solve a problem, imagine connecting with the part who is trying to figure it out, letting it know you see how hard it is working. My figure it out part is busy and active. I feel her in my head and in the squint of my eyes.

It is ironic, but we all know it is true: you need to settle the mind down in order for an idea to come forward. You are trying to think of a word and you can't until two hours later when you are not even thinking about it. Clarity does not typically come until there is more space.

For More Connection Today

Think of a time recently where you had a lot of chatter in your head. Now you know those are parts talking to you. Get curious about one of those parts. Begin to imagine leaning back from that part as if you were holding a pillow at arm's length in order to see it more clearly. Stay with that until you experience more clarity with this part. What does it look like, sound like, feel like? How does it feel different to you with this clarity? Say "Hello," smile, and see what it wants you to know.

DAY 11 — *Courage*

It takes courage to lean in and get to know our parts. It takes courage to focus on what our parts are saying and what they are intending for us. It takes courage to do this work. It takes courage to feel, which is often the exact thing we are avoiding. It takes courage to turn toward our parts because we do not know what they will say, what they know, or what will happen next.

It takes courage to go toward parts who are not likeable, such as our internal Critic. Often our critical parts are trying to keep us from feeling shame, not knowing the critique itself causes shame.

I just heard a part say, "But not as bad as if we didn't; feeling my own critique is easier then feeling the shame of being criticized by others."

One of the things which makes us resistant to listen to our parts is we are afraid we will see, feel, and be confronted with our own badness, our shame.

Let's return to the parts who chatted yesterday when I was on the paddleboard. Since I worked with the Figure-It-Out part, I have more space to hear from the other two. I am especially curious about the Critic

as it is a familiar voice, one I hear often. The two other voices are the one who told me I had gone too far and the one who told it to shut up.

Another part of me is Worried about what I will uncover or if I will be flooded with emotion. I let it know it is okay, it does not need to be around for this, and I remind it I have courage to talk with them.

I turn my attention first to the one who told it to Shut Up, knowing the first one will not be open if it feels criticized. This one tells me that it doesn't want my time to be ruined, it is a beautiful day and it knows how much I want to enjoy it. It believes the other one will take that away from me. Okay, that makes a lot of sense. I let it know that and thank it for watching out for me. It likes that and settles back, giving me space to focus on the first voice.

This one says, "You always do this. You knew the wind was bad, you don't think about the time. What is wrong with you? You are going to get in trouble because you will be later than expected. And then your day will be ruined."

I notice this part looks like an old-fashioned School Teacher with glasses, pointing her finger at me. She seems gruff and angry at me.

"Oh, okay. So, you also don't want my day ruined? Wow, thank you for looking out for me," I say to it feeling an openness to it.

After getting acknowledged and appreciated, this part begins to show me other times in my life when this happened. When I didn't track time and then experienced getting in trouble, which led to thoughts of being bad and feeling shame. It is trying to help me not feel shame. I continue letting it know what it is doing makes sense given that information.

Notice what it would be like for you to ask a part you have gotten to know over the past few days about how and when it has showed up in your life. Stay with open curiosity as it shows you. Notice if there are any parts who do not want you to ask this. Courage is a C quality of Self, and when you are feeling that hesitancy or fear, ask inside what part is up and what it wants you to know.

For More Connection Today

 Courage is inside of you, even when parts cannot accept it or do not believe it. Notice what came up as you were listening to my parts dialogue. Do you have a similar dialogue you can track? If one part seems to be criticizing another part, ask it to give space. This one will be your **target part,** the one who holds information about how and why it is protecting you.

Begin to track what this voice sounds like; what it feels like in your body when it is driving the bus. You may even notice how other parts respond to it. Remember this target part is the one in the spotlight so continue asking parts to give space so you can focus and be with it. Remind your parts you have the courage to be with them all in Self.

DAY 12 — *Doing*

Yesterday, I got to know a manager, the teacher, who shows up with a critical voice and tone.

We have already met a few of my managers; they are busy and have specific agendas. They are focused on doing, helping, and organizing. They often think they are me and, although they are exhausted by their job, they believe they have to do it. They work hard to make sure I do not feel the upset and intense feelings of my exiles.

One of my managers likes to always put things back in the Same Spot. My keys go in this specific pocket on my bag and my son's belt goes back on a hanger every day after school. I realized this was a manager when the belt was not on the hanger in the morning. I felt my heart begin to race as I rushed around the house. I heard two things that stood out to me:

1) We are wasting time looking for this belt;
2) What kind of mom would I be if he went to school without a belt?

I recognized by the intensity behind these questions and the panic reaction in my body when this happened, that my manager orders my life so I don't have to feel these ways. Managers work ahead of time so we do not feel the experience of our exiles.

Another example of a much-loved manager is one who has So Many Ideas to help me feel worthy. I can make a guess that she is protecting an exile does not feel valuable or worthwhile.

If I am painting a house, a part shouts out, "You know what would be a great idea? We should rip all the wallpaper off the bathroom wall!" And you know what, it is a good idea and something I'd like to do. But I don't need that suggestion *right now*. I certainly don't need to put down the paint brush, climb down from the ladder, and go into my bathroom to start ripping off wallpaper.

These are similar to managers I have spoken about before. I have a good amount of energy and focus, and they want me to be efficient and effective with it. So, I will ask it to remind me later or write it down.

Slowing down is a great way to begin to connect to my managers. I need to slow down my body and mind. I need to pause in order to hear inside. Up on that ladder painting the house, I can still do this. Slowing down my mind though, taking a breath so I am more embodied with Self, I can hear what is happening inside.

When I don't slow down to hear what my parts are saying, I feel like I *am* that part because I am blended. I would most likely run down off the ladder (probably fall off of it because I am moving so fast).

When I bring this slowness to my internal parts, I am more likely to notice what part I am hearing. If I am slow, I can recognize a part who brings up past hurts and causes me to stew. When I am not slow, I can get lost in the icky, sticky, chucky stew. Gross.

But slowly, I am able to hear and, in listening, I unblend to bring more of my Self into my system.

Many are familiar with the idea of non-doing that is often spoken about in yoga classes. I remember the first time I heard this. I attended a conference once and they began with a meditation which started with "There is nowhere to go, nothing to do," and I started crying. Well, balling really, the snot running down my face, sobbing completely. This was a revolutionary idea and it continues to be one of my favorite statements. This concept that I can just be, right here, right now is an anomaly to my system.

When I listen inside I also hear this: "Nothing to do and nobody I have to be."

That is interesting. It appears a part of me has equated Doing with Being. If I do enough, I am enough. "Oh, Hi, sweetheart. I hear you. I see you. You are enough."

I'm going to sit right here with this part, get to know her, and let her feel me with her.

As I do this, I notice an immediate ease in my body. I'm not blended with one of my doing managers any longer. I am able to get ideas and information on her intentions and motivations.

I notice an ease in my facial muscles and in my body. The wrinkle between my brows has disappeared as my face is not as tense. My body is at ease. I am slower in movements and in thoughts.

For More Connection Today

 Connect with one of your To-Do manager parts. What is it trying to keep you from experiencing? Ask what it fears would happen if it was not so busy, or however it shows up for you. Notice how it helps you organize your life, your relationships, and your schedule to keep you from activating an exile. Listen with your heart and ask your thinking mind to give you space. What is happening in your body as you unblend from these parts? Remind the parts you are not trying to get rid of them. You want to build a friendship with them.

DAY 13 Compassion

We see how our managers work hard to anticipate the emotion of an exile. Today, we will meet the category of parts who helps us when the emotion of the exile is triggered. This feeling can be described as a fire, and we need a Firefighter to put it out. This sounds like a good idea, but our Firefighter parts are often the ones who get us in trouble. They are often our addicted parts.

They are the ones who cause a lot of damage, just like a firefighter may have to break down the front door to the house to save the people inside. Once that fire has started, the firefighter will do what it needs to do in order to put that fire out.

Another one of my favorite C words of Self is **compassion.** It is often hard to bring compassion to your firefighter parts when they are acting up or behaving in ways other parts of you do not like.

When we begin to see all parts as protecting us in some way then we can begin to have compassion. Often parts have anger, guilt, and shame about our firefighter behaviors. We see the firefighters are just trying hard to put out the fire.

Our firefighter parts are trying hard to protect the hurt that resides in our younger, vulnerable, scared parts of us inside. Compassion can expand to more of our system when we understand and appreciate what they are trying to do.

Another way to expand compassion is by understanding all of your parts have a good reason for doing what they do. They have your best interest at heart. Their behaviors have or had a function in the past which helped you survive. They have learned to do what they do in order to protect you. They all think they have the best idea to provide help and to keep the vulnerable emotions (exiled parts) and their big emotions away from you.

Once the hurt and pain is triggered, the fire has started. The firefighters will use whatever means they have to extinguish the fire, the hurt and pain immediately.

A good example of a common Firefighter of mine is the part who Eats All the Cookies. I notice the part who likes to joke and make light of this part in order to not experience shame. My beloved Cookie-Eater is active when I am feel unheard, unseen, and angry. These experiences are intense, like a hot fire and I do not feel emotionally safe.

Another way of saying this is when a younger part of me feels unheard and unseen, another part eats a lot of cookies to help us feel better.

I remember a time recently when I was with someone I did not know very well. She was talking non-stop and sharing interesting things about her life. I felt numb and disconnected, as if I wasn't actually there. After I dropped her off to get gas, I felt this intense need to go into the gas station store and buy junk food. It felt like an emergency. I gobbled up the sweet treats quickly and then felt myself exhale. I felt better. The emergency was over.

There was a part who felt Embarrassed by this, it was not like I made a healthy, thoughtful choice in that gas station. There was a part who felt Confused. I was not sure what happened or why I had this strong urge to do that.

All I know for certain is a part said I needed to eat immediately in order to be present. Later, I recognized a part felt Invisible and another part was Trying to Help. This Junk Food Eater part was trying to help me, and I, Self, have compassion for this part and let it know I see how it was trying to help. I let it know that I see it and I also see the part who did not feel seen in that conversation.

When we have compassion for our firefighter parts, we are more open to hear their story and they are more open to tell it. If all our firefighters feel from us is fear, anger, and shame, they will shut down. They will also shut us down by causing us to dissociate, numb out, or go blank. This is how we typically treat our addicted parts; we try to hide, ignore, blame, and hate them. We just need them to stop what they are doing and we try to beat them into submission. This does not work.

Compassion helps our firefighter parts soften and allows for more open communication. When we offer compassion, we begin to have a relationship together, so those parts do not hijack us or overwhelm us. We can hear about who they are trying to protect and go to that part to help it. When Self becomes the protector, the one to take care of the younger parts, our firefighters can rest.

Remembering firefighter's function helps us bring compassion to these hard-to-love-parts. It had an important function in the past and maybe still does in the present.

These parts function to soothe me, help me, assure my survival, continue my growth, and make sure I succeed. They keep the overwhelming feelings of the exile at bay. They are blinded to the consequences of their actions; they are only here to perform an important function and they do an amazing job.

When I see a part that I don't like as having a role in my system, I can have more compassion for it. Then there is more space between me and this part so I can see it more clearly and get to know it.

Who are your firefighters? What are their behaviors? What do they tell you? Look inside with soft curiosity. Once you have gotten to know your go-to firefighters' roles and functions, ask it a series of questions from your open heart: What were its original functions? Why does it think it still needs to do that? Does it know how old you are now? Would it like to have another job if it could learn to trust you? Can it introduce you to the one it is protecting?

For More Connection Today

 Who are your hard to like parts, the parts who over-eat, sleep, drink, shop, spend time online, gossip? Who are the parts who become overly judgmental and critical of yourself and others, who obsess, try to control things, or work too much? Who are the parts you keep in secret or feel embarrassed about? Identify one and walk through some questions above. Imagine this part initially had a helpful function.

An actual firefighter is only concerned about putting out the fire even if this means destroying the house and taking an axe to the front door in order to rescue you from the flames. Practice showing some appreciation or acknowledgment for its hard work.

DAY 14 — *Cathartic*

I introduced you to a part of me on Day 10 who said, "You will get in trouble, you will feel shame, and your day will be ruined." I have information and history now about this part and want to explore it more. It says it is anticipating trouble and trying to keep me away from it. I have tracked how this part shows up in my life. Now, I want to ask it what or who it is trying to protect.

I understand it is a manager part protecting an exiled part. This exiled part holds a lot of feelings that the manager tries to hold back, afraid those feelings will flood the system.

As I focus on the School Teacher pointing, I put my attention on her until she notices me. I see if she can step away from me a bit, letting her feel my curiosity and open heart and I ask, "What are you afraid would happen if you didn't do this?"

It responds: "Your partner will be mad at you."

And what would happen then? "You will get mad at him."

And then what? "You won't talk to each other."

And then what? "You will feel sad."

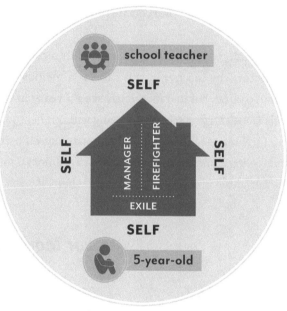

And then what? "You will feel alone."

And then what? "You will be alone."

This cathartic, ah-ha moment is almost indescribable. It comes from this understanding of why this protective part of me has been working so hard and for so long. From this daisy-chain like questioning I get an idea of what she fears and who inside of me she is trying to protect, the one who feels alone.

A part of me feels Alone, and the School Teacher is trying to help me from ever feeling it. This is a younger, vulnerable, fragile part who has been exiled away from me so I don't have to experience this feeling ever. The Teacher works very hard to make sure I do not.

A few things may happen now.

I can ask the Teacher to introduce me to the one inside who feels lonely. I can just ask it this way: "Can you show me inside who you are protecting, who feels so lonely?"

What often happens organically after meeting the protector (the teacher in this case) is a memory will come to mind. For instance, I may see a 5-year-old who feels alone starting school and being without her mom.

Or, I may see this younger version of myself being and feeling alone without a context of a memory. I may see her alone in a corner of a room by herself.

Another great question to help identify what the protector is protecting is to ask it how old it thinks you are. Often it believes you are the same age as the part it is protecting. In this case, the teacher may think I am 5 years old, or at least it thinks I am much younger. It sees me as young and needing protecting. It does not see me as my actual age and in the context of my current life. We will talk more about updating later but for now try this question: How old do you think I am?

As soon as my attention and focus move from the protector, the School Teacher, the one I hear in my head, to the one she is protecting, I feel a softening in my body and curiosity toward this younger part. I am ready to meet and interact with her.

For More Connection Today

 Ask your target part what it is afraid would happen if it didn't do what it is doing and see what it says. And then ask: "And then what would happen?" a few times until the worst case is realized. Take your time. Go slowly. You've got this. See if it will tell you who inside it is protecting.

Phase Two:
Trailheads

DAY 15 · *Morning*

One of my favorite habits for connecting to my parts is greeting them in the morning. Having a morning ritual of some kind is a well-known practice to help establish the tone of your day, whether that is exercise, meditation, or doing the *NY Times* Crossword puzzle.

I heard an author say the best time for writing or any creativity happens in the morning. I am sure some would disagree as everyone has different rhythms to their energy during the day. Nevertheless, it is important to know your cycle; when you have the most access to creativity.

Since creativity is a C word, this may be a time you have more access to Self-energy. Another way to think about this is to consider the time of day when your protectors (the parts who use the chatter in your head to get your attention) are less active when you don't have to work so hard to unblend from them in order to have Self emerge.

Imagine parts covering your true essence, yourSelf. We ask them to unblend and they step aside by moving away or giving you space so that you can experience Self, which is behind them all along. We talked about this on Day Two with the clouds covering the sun.

Think of other times of the day or situations when parts are less active. Some of those times for me are outside in nature, exercising, and connecting to warm, kind people. These are times I know my parts are covering me less because I do not need as much protection, and I have more access to Self.

Another way to think of having more access to Self is to think of Self as a Spirit in you who can flow into your thoughts, feelings, and bodily sensations. The more you feed it, the more it grows and expands. The more you spend time in it, the more access you have to it. I imagine my Spirit reaching out from my heart up to my head and down to my fingers and to my toes as if it is water or air flowing inside. It feels like it takes up more of me.

Morning is ripe for this experience. I feel freer of part energy so I can have more creativity. Part energy will feel different for each part and each person. You are probably beginning to get a sense of it though as you get to know Self, you will get to know what part energy feels like, too.

I can sense my Self before my managers wake up and start telling me all the things I need to do. Sometimes this may only last for a half of a second! However, I have noticed it can be a time to check in with my parts and let them know I am here before I even get out of bed.

It is a powerful way to connect to them, to let them know I am here and listening before we start the day. This is a great practice to start. Your parts begin to trust you are listening and open to hear from them throughout the day.

I took a walk this morning and thought about the book I read to my son last night, *Goodnight Moon*. I began saying Good mornin' to all the things I saw. I happened to be in Florida right then so it sounded like this: Good morning, sunrise; Good morning, palm trees; Good morning, seagull; Good morning, jumping fish; Good morning, feet hitting the pavement; Good morning, breath.

How could your mornings be different, less parts-driven, and more Self-led if you said, "Good morning, bed," as you made it? "Good morning, shower," as the warm water hit your shoulders. "Good morning, fridge," as you made you and/or your family's meals. "Good morning, keys" as you ran out to the car.

Now, try saying "Good Morning" to the parts who are up already: Good morning, Planner. Good morning, Figure It Out. Good morning, Why Didn't I go to Bed Earlier Last Night. Good morning, Critic of my body and my clothes. Good morning, Everyone who works so hard to help me. I see you.

This is one way to allow parts to soften and Self to emerge as you start your day. You can let your parts know you want to hear from them. There is plenty of time. Greeting the day and your parts this way reminds them that you are here and you are listening. It also reminds you to slow and be a bit more present.

Starting the morning this way with an openness to your parts allows you to be aware of the trailheads you may encounter throughout the day. More on this tomorrow!

For More Connection Today

 Practice saying Good Mornin'! as you rise and begin your day. Look for small details outside of you and inside of you to greet. Greet the parts you know about, greet the parts who are up, and greet what you see around you. Notice the feeling of Self emerging and expanding. Notice if you have any resistance to these ideas and check in with soft curiosity about that. Notice if you have other creative ideas to help you begin to establish a pattern for checking in with your parts.

DAY 16 · *Wait*

Trailheads mark the beginning of a path. Where I live in New Hampshire, I can drive on most any highway in the White Mountains and notice a line of cars on the side of the road. They are parked at trailheads.

A trailhead may not look like much; it may even look scary or threatening. But if you take the trailhead that leads down a path and you make your way through the woods, you may find yourself at a glorious waterfall or summitting a mountain with gorgeous views all around.

Exploring a trailhead, even if the path is steep and rocky and you are out of breath, is worth the pay off at the top. If you take this path, opening to whatever messages a part is telling you, you will find your way to the waterfall. It can be the emotional pay off of deep listening inside and a heart-felt connection to Self.

Try using the term **trailhead** instead of the term trigger. If I think of triggers as trailheads, I am more apt to have curiosity toward my reactions instead of focusing on and blaming the cause. For example, if my son does not pick up his toys even if I have asked him one zillion times, a part of me may yell at him "Pick up your TOYS!"

I can focus on him and his lack of listening as the trigger to my outburst or I can focus in on my own reaction with curiosity and compassion. I can do a "You-Turn," focusing on my own experience.

A common trailhead for me is being interrupted. Parts of me work hard to prevent this by talking fast and not allowing for pauses for fear I will be interrupted. This happened recently during a light-hearted chat with a close friend. I noticed a part Shut Down and wanted to leave immediately and another part who wanted to Scream.

Instead of focusing on feeling angry and hurt toward my friend, I wanted to use this as an opportunity to learn more about my own system. I also wanted to get to know my shut down and angry parts and the parts of me (exiles) they are protecting.

Waiting is another trailhead for me. I don't like waiting and notice parts will take me out of these experiences in a variety of ways.

There are a few types of waiting. Waiting in the grocery store line, waiting to learn something new or gain a new skill, and waiting for someone else to change or grow.

What happens inside of you when you need to or are forced to wait? Check inside as you read this and notice what comes up. What do you hear in your head? What do you feel in your body? Think about the last time you were waiting for a friend to meet you or waiting in line, what did you do? You most likely looked at your phone. It can be difficult and it is not uncommon to feel uncomfortable and hard to tolerate.

What I hear inside if I have to wait: This is a waste of our time, Why don't they hurry up, We could have been doing something else.

I notice a part who feels impatient and another who begins to feel annoyed. This becomes the point of growth for me. I want to get to know the part of me who says, "This is a waste of my time!"

I can cultivate gratitude for these triggers and trailheads as they help me get to know parts of my system.

I also have parts who react to waiting for goals to be met. For instance, if I work out for a day (or maybe a week) I don't understand why I haven't lost 20 lbs. and don't yet have tight abs. Waiting for results can be tough. I want to get to know this part who wants results now and feels impatient.

It is also hard to wait to learn something new or to form sustainable habits. It's hard to wait to hear from a someone, for another person to change, or for a relationship to heal. I want all that right now. Well, a part of me does.

It is hard to wait your turn. A part of me is eager to ask a question or to share information. It is excited to have a turn to share its thoughts and feelings. I want others to hurry up so I get to have my turn to be heard and to share.

I want to listen to all the parts around waiting. I notice there are few and they have different feelings depending on the circumstances. But I notice a common theme: they want something now and they are physically uncomfortable when they do not get it. I notice my hands move to my hips, my foot begins to tap, and the voice in my head saying, "Let's get going people!"

Think of a time you felt triggered by someone else or something in your environment. Look at this as a trailhead, as an opportunity for growth and healing. What parts of you were activated?

For More Connection Today

 What do your parts want to say to you about the different areas of your life where waiting is hard? One thing I know is the parts who come up around waiting are young and desire instant gratification. Not getting it now feels like not being able to get it at all, ever. How would you talk to a child who wants all the M-and-M's right now instead of waiting for the full course meal of chicken nuggets and pizza *and* chocolate cake? This is how you would approach and be with those parts.

It is hard to wait for our parts to unblend, heal, and transform. This work can be slow. There is irony in this process because the slower we go with our parts, the faster the results, the quicker the healing. I have a part who is impatient with working with other parts saying, "Why can't we be in Self all the time?"

Working with your parts who have a hard time waiting may help your whole system. Softening the impatient parts may open space for connection with other parts. Let them know you get how they feel, you understand the rush to heal and feel better. Negotiate some space and ask them to watch how this goes differently when they let you take the lead, even if this means going at a slower pace.

Maybe waiting is not a trailhead for you. What did you notice as you read about You-Turns, trailheads and waiting? Is there a trail here you can follow?

DAY 17 — *Occupied*

Worry is a trailhead as it can rob us of our joy, of being present, and of connection with others. I notice parts who do not like worry and other parts who say worry is "natural, everyone worries." I want to bring curiosity to the parts of me who worry and notice when they interrupt my life.

My son was hypnotized by a dead fish I scooped out of the water with his net and put on my paddleboard. He was so occupied with admiring and poking it, he no longer was mad that I had left the goldfish snacks in the car or upset that we had yet to catch any fish. Well, we had not caught any fish alive.

There is wonder on a child's face when they experience something new, something wonderful. Or, in this case something gross. The brightness, the awe, the focus on this one thing. My son was not thinking about the frustration of the past five hours. All of that stopped as he looked at this fish.

By looking at him and being with him, I experienced the same thing. I was no longer hearing the parts of me who had been so activated: annoyed with him for complaining, begging the fish to snag his line, criticizing myself for forgetting the goldfish. I was no longer planning where we would stop on the way home and what time we needed to leave in order to be home in time for his bath and to get ready for the next day.

I was feeling more Self energy as my body mirrored his. I was light, open, calm, and focused. The focus was in watching the wonder on his little face as he poked the dead, smelly fish.

What parts keep you from wonder by being occupied by other thoughts? I know my parts are often going so fast and are too prone to overthinking to experience wonder. They tell me we don't have time or they want to numb out or distract from unpleasant emotions. They tell me they are sick and tired of my feelings and everyone else's and want a break.

Maybe your parts tell you something about the world being too hard, too dark, too terrible. So they try to keep you from being present to wonder.

What the mind is occupied with will direct how we feel. Consider this: Is your mind occupied by wonder or worry?

An inhibiter to wonder is worry. Worry is meditating on all the stuff that is, was, and could be wrong with you, other people, and the world. It is one way to occupy your mind; it blocks you from experiencing your life. This may be a part's intention; when you worry you do not have to experience your life. Keeping you disconnected could be one of the part's positive intentions.

Perhaps it is a way a part of you learned to cope. Maybe it is a way a part of you feels like it can have control or a way a part of you learned to interact with others. Maybe it is a part who equates worry with love. Remember your parts always have a function.

Worry is such a waste of your energy (says a part of me). When someone tells me they are worried about their brother who just lost his job, I'm not sure if my concern should be for the brother or them. I wonder if they have equated worry with care and if they feel less helpless by their worry. I am curious about their worry parts.

Check inside and see how your Worrier parts are reacting to this. They may tell you they are right: worry does help you feel more in control. Of course they think they are right! If this resonates, smile and let them know you hear them and you understand their positive intention for you.

Worry is often a drain on our time and energy. Does it help the situation or the person? No. Is it effective? No. With what would you like to occupy your mind? Do you notice what is actually taking up space in your thoughts? Is worry a space holder of sorts, keeping you from thinking of other things? Bring in curiosity and see what happens.

There may be times that worry is a part's strategy and it is the best choice at the time. A part is using it as a needed distraction or to keep you away from feeling helpless. But you would like to have this information and to be with those parts who are feeling this way.

When I think of worry, I often think of prayer and meditation. I was told growing up, "If you can worry, you can pray." Prayer and meditation have many emotional and spiritual benefits. Meditation can be as simple as noticing where your attention lands. Are you meditating on worries? If so, go to that part and be curious about how it is trying to help.

Your mind can be occupied by saying a verse, a poem, a song, an intention, or a mantra. Or it can be steeped in worries and fears. What is it like when you are occupied with a song in your head? Your whole body feels different. Does a part draw you back to worry? Bring curiosity to this part; it may teach you how it believes it is helping by occupying your mind in this way.

For More Connection Today

Bring curiosity to these parts and ask them to give space so you can get to know them. Ask them what they are afraid would happen if they let you just be in the now in order to look around today with wondering eyes.

How do you experience wonder? Set an intention to notice wonder around and inside of you. Notice what gets in your way or stops you, what parts interfere. Notice what parts take you out of presence, the parts who do not allow you to stay in the moment.

DAY 18 · *Honest*

One way I know I am blended with a part is when I over use the word "Fine" as in "I'm fine, everything is fine, we are all fine." The overuse, or the use at all of this word is a cue I am in a part.

A part of me says I am not honest when I do this. When people ask me how I am doing, I respond, "I'm fine. How are you?" This part is a major player in my system, and I call her Fine.

I value honesty. I won't lie about pretty much anything. But I will lie about my feelings over and over. Now, I don't mean when the nice lady who is walking her dogs asks, "Good morning! How are you today?" I am going to tell her about my cat who just died and I just found out I owe money on an old credit card. But if my friend, my husband, or my mom asks how I am or if my feelings are hurt, am I going to be honest or am I going to pretend?

I have a very powerful, wonderful part who has pretended she is Fine, that I am fine, for a very long time. Because I believe strongly that I value honesty, I know she must have a good reason for being an active part of my system.

When I check in with her with curiosity, she says she thought this kept people happy and me emotionally safe. She has a fear that if she tells someone she feels a certain way, they will tell her why she is wrong to feel that way, making her feel worse.

When I was little and someone asked me if I wanted something to drink, I always said, "No, Thank you." I was always thirsty so the chances are I actually wanted to say "Yes." My mother overheard me once and gave me permission to accept by telling me it was not rude to accept. I thought I always had to be fine in order to be loved, even when it came to basic needs like thirst.

In order for me to be honest now about my feelings, I need to get to know Fine and help her with these fears. As I connect to Fine by putting attention on the numbness I feel when she is blended with me, I hear her say she believes she is too needy, she will upset someone else if she shares her feelings or asks for what she needs.

I let her know she does not have to be the one to speak to how I feel. I can do that. She is younger and she would rather be playing with dolls, not telling adults how she feels.

Another part reminds me her fears are also around the need to defend my feelings. A part feels frightened of having to give a defense because we don't know how hard the other person will push back. I notice another part's anger toward this part. It finds her embarrassing and weak.

I let them all know I hear this. I understand their points and their reactions to each other. I smile at all of them and let them know their reactions make sense.

Another aspect of this is that my Fine part has strong numbing capabilities. Sometimes I actually don't know how I feel; I actually just feel fine because this Fine part has blocked all other feelings.

I ask her to let me stay with whatever is coming up, to stay present with whatever is happening. I reassure her that some feelings may be hard to handle for her, and I can handle them instead.

My Fine part works hard to find ways to not stay in my feelings. Sometimes it uses a side show to distract me by focusing on gossip, criticizing others, making light of a situation, or being silly. I let her know I see how she is trying to help me by distracting me in order to protect me from big feelings. I ask her, "What are you afraid would happen if I just stay, stay with whatever I am feeling?"

I hear, "It is dangerous. I would have to defend and explain myself. I will be minimized or dismissed. I will be invalidated and made fun of. I am too sensitive to handle this. It is easier to smile, be polite, and eat cookies later."

I let her know this makes a lot of sense and thank her for how hard she works for me.

I'm curious what is happening for you as you read this. Do you have a Fine part? Maybe yours is called Numb or Distracted. Maybe you have a strong Assertive part who believes she has to be louder and more extreme in order to be heard. Be curious about what parts of you are up around expressing yourself.

For More Connection Today

Notice what you "lie" about, especially around sharing your feelings with your support systems. Who is afraid and what are they afraid of? Name this part. Get to know this part of you with compassion and gentleness. Notice what this part tends to use as a distraction so you don't stay with big feelings. Remind them you can take on this job and stay with hard feelings. Ask what they would rather do.

DAY 19 · *Freedom*

"You should wear the black skirt with the red shirt. Eat the oatmeal and save the eggs for tomorrow. Go to the coffee shop for lunch because the sandwich place is closed Mondays. Oh, wait. You need to get a card and present for sister so maybe you should pack your lunch and go to the store. The boy needs that permission slip signed and you forgot to get him to fill out his homework sheet. Okay, do that before you give him breakfast."

I hear all of this in my mind before I even open my eyes. This compulsive planning part chats inside of me as soon as I am aware of the birds singing outside my window.

Parts of me love this part. It is helpful, organized, and it helps me think through things and be well prepared. I am not someone who tends to forget things because of the hypervigilance of this part. I'm effective because my inner Administrative Assistant, which I call my Secretary, works so hard for me.

But, heavens to betsy it is enough already (say other parts). "Madam Secretary," they reply sarcastically, "Does not shut up, turn off, or stop!"

I ask both camps, the one who loves her and the one who does not, to step aside, to give us some space so I can get to know Secretary.

What I desire, and what I believe my parts desire is choice and freedom around when she is going to show up and how extreme she will be. Freedom to be able to choose how loud this voice is going to be. I still need her at times but, I want to control the dial so I can turn her up at times and turn her down at others.

This is true for so many of our protective parts: they play incredible roles in our life but do so with an unbearable intensity often due to polarized parts and the exiled part they are protecting.

I connect with her by noticing the rapid-fire instructions in my head. I smile and say "Hello." I ask her to separate from me so I can get to know her better and see her with more clarity. I let her know how much I appreciate her, but it becomes difficult because her volume drowns out other parts. I let her know it often feels like a lot of noise and I cannot even distinguish the points she is trying to make.

This assures her of my appreciation for her skills and strategies. Now, I can listen to what she wants me to know. I ask her two essential questions with curiosity and compassion: What is she trying to do for me? and What is she concerned would happen if she did not do that?

She lets me know she wants to keep me organized and successful. She is afraid we will become lazy. If we become "too lazy," we will be unlovable.

I thank her and ask her if there is a way she can communicate with me in a different way. We begin to negotiate, and we decide together to write things down that she is telling me for later when I'm ready and able to do something with the information she gives me. She wants me to listen to her and likes that I will attune to her by writing down her ideas.

My system quiets with this. Parts are hesitantly watching to see how this goes, the parts who like her and parts who do not. Ultimately, I know I want to help The One Inside who feels unlovable, she is the one the Secretary is protecting. With helping the part (the exile) who is unlovable, Secretary will be able to do her job differently.

For More Connection Today

 Do you have a similar part to the Secretary? What did you notice as you read the above passage for today? What parts resonated and what parts offered other examples from your own system?

Invite them around a table or imagine handing them a talking stick. Can they pass it around the circle with confidence that when they are holding the stick they have your attention? Let them know they will all get a turn with you.

What does your planning part sound like and how often do you hear it? Or, do you have a part who struggles with planning? How are you feeling toward it? Let it know and see how it reacts. Consider negotiating with it so you have a strategy that works for everyone.

When a part becomes too loud, practice playing with the volume nob. Let it know you want to hear it and you want freedom to adjust the nob. Let it know you can actually hear it more clearly.

DAY 20 *Soften*

I love vacation: the break from my routine, the new surroundings, the slower pace. As much as I love vacation, I despise returning from one. It feels like a hard shift, an abrupt turn full of overwhelming responsibilities and obligations. It can be a trailhead for sure.

On vacation I feel a softening in my body. I feel more embodied and connected. I feel lighter and I seem to get a break from my overworking managers who run my non-vacation life.

I like to think about what I do, feel, and think on vacation that I can bring into my normal life. Obviously, I can't bring in sitting on the beach all day, reading books, and napping in the sun. I let a part know there are moments of this I can intentionally put into my life. A part says, "If only some other parts will let you."

Vacation is often a great time out for me to reconsider what I want the flow of my day-to-day life to be like and start to be curious about my parts. Some parts of me are softer on vacation (like a part concerned about deadlines) and there are other parts of me who are softer when I am at home (like the parts who want to make the best use of the time). I can also think about parts who are softer on the weekends or my days off and the parts who are softer during the work week.

My manager parts are softer on vacation. My Clipboard Manager is taking a nap. My parts know they are not needed in the same way. They think differently about time, tasks, and goals. My daily home goals involve getting 1,000 things done simultaneously while being with my family. My weekly vacation goals are to notice, to enjoy, to be with the moment.

I like to think of what is true and real and consistently there when I return from vacation. My family, my faith, my hobbies. How can I be with those things in the routines of life as I am when I am vacationing? On vacation I am more present, I take time to pray and to spend time with God, I read—a lot! I make time to paddleboard, to do a puzzle, to just sit with my son and play Legos on the floor. There is more connection with my family, emotionally, and physically.

All of these can be done at home but not in the same way. I can bring in a slower mindset, taking one moment at a time, not thinking too far ahead. I can let the day play out a little more in front of me instead of trying to control and track every minute of my time.

My Take Advantage of Each Moment parts are softer when I am at home. I am not trying to maximize every minute. I do not think as often, "What would feel good to me right now?" Or, "How do I want to spend this time?" It is just as important to notice the parts who come forward when your Hard-Working Manager parts relax again.

You may be thinking, "But in life, we don't have time for those things!"

To that I say, "Bologna."

We have time for that which we make time. How much time did you spend today looking at your smartphone? Or watching television or movies and videos online? You do something in your day to zone out, we all do. That is great because it means you have time to soften.

We can all make time to be intentional about something. Whether it is spending more time with friends or family, with your favorite hobby, with relaxing in whatever way feels right and good for you, there is no reason you cannot do this.

The parts who are softer on vacation don't need to be protecting you as much or in the same way. At home, in normal life they are more activated and needed.

Life looks different at home. I read an hour a night, not eight hours in a day. I paddleboard once a week in the early morning and maybe take my son to the beach on a Saturday. The dishes and laundry can wait. I'll have a vague sense and plan of what needs to be done that day and week.

My parts think differently about time and tasks, about how they define productivity and the day's value. This is why this is a great trailhead for me as it involves how and when my parts allow me to relax, have fun, and enjoy life.

For More Connection Today

 Who are you on vacation or when you are able to get away from your daily routine? How is that different than your day-to-day life? What elements can you begin to bring into your day and week? What behaviors and mind shift changes can you start implementing? What parts inside react to this? What do you hear as you read this and how can you soothe and reassure those parts?

Pay attention to who softens inside during vacation. How do you experience them differently? Do you hear them differently in your mind? Do you feel the pull to be busy in your body? Do you feel less rushed?

Mine soften on the plane ride down and use a megaphone to wake me up on the plane ride back. I can be with these parts and help them use their power in my system differently. I love the gifts that they bring and I let them know. As I do, we can begin to shift our relationship. As you notice this part inside of you, your relationship with Self will shift, too.

DAY 21 · *Confidence*

One of the biggest trailheads to get to know our own parts is found in our relationships. When we begin to look at the parts who show up in our relationships as invitations to learn about our systems, we can begin to observe our reactions. This keeps us from blaming and focusing on others.

I encourage you to think of a You-Turn when it comes to the dance of relationships. With a You-Turn, I am turning inside to look at my own parts who are activated instead of pointing the finger at others in blame and in defensiveness.

I am also very aware of others' parts. Knowing we are multiple helps us realize that everyone else is, too! I adore the funny, wise, and thoughtful parts of my husband. I don't especially adore the perfectionistic and sarcastic ones. Understanding and seeing my husband as having protective parts, younger exiles, and a Self has made a huge difference in how I see, relate, and connect to him.

As I check in with my system when I think about the significant relationships in my life, I hear a part say I need more **confidence** to be able to connect, to share my feelings, and to be vulnerable.

Sometimes we don't know how to say what we want, or what we want to say does not come out the way we intended. It is messy. I have parts who just avoid it all together and who tell me, "It is easier, safer, less complex just to keep it all in." But other parts know it is often more damaging to our relationships to do this.

Let's use a fun, light example to demonstrate: your partner brings you coffee in a fall mug when it is summer. You love mugs and have favorites for every season. A part of you does not want to say anything. "This is silly, they are being nice. You are being picky and ridiculous."

Another part of you may think, "It's the little things. It is important to me, and they would want to know." This part feels confident in this. But other parts do not because they have believed for a long time that your needs are not as important as other people's.

One problem with not saying something is a part of you may build up some mild irritations; first at him and then at yourself. You may notice this creates a disconnection between you and even an energy shift: your partner smiles as they bring you coffee with excited energy and you give them a phony smile with a lower energetic response back.

If a part of you doesn't feel comfortable saying something about this light, smaller matter, then this part definitely is not going to say something in heavier matters.

A part of you may be thinking, "But this does not matter. I will speak up for the weightier issues." Maybe. Check inside and see if that feels true for you.

Remember that confidence is a C word, a Self quality that you do have even when parts of you do not feel this way. Think about a way you struggle with confidence in your relationship. It may show up differently for you and in your system.

One metaphor that helps me think through difficult communication is the three-legged stool used in Dialectical Behavioral Therapy (DBT) to teach relationship effectiveness. Picture a stool where all three legs need to be the same length in order for it to stand and be balanced.

The parts of me who get in the way of implementing the three legs of the stool do it for good reason. It is important to remember that my parts have a function and my protection as their goal. As you read about the stool and the role of each leg to hold it steady, notice which parts tell you it is too hard, it won't work, or who get defensive or hesitate. Those voices are important ones to note and get to know better.

The first leg is self-respect: Can I say this in a way that holds to my values such as honesty, humility, and owning what I have contributed? Yelling, blaming,

or ignoring and giving the silent treatment are not respectful of me (not just the other person). Acting too small or too big are also not respectful to my system and neither is minimizing or exaggerating to get my needs met. I want to pay attention to what a part believes about who I need to be and how I need to behave.

The second leg is relationship: consider the intensity, history, and role of this person in my life. I am probably not going to say anything if the stranger at the checkout line rolls their eyes at me. But I may. The connection I have with the other person matters. I may say something to the stranger but I may not say something to a close family member. It is important to think through the value and type of relationship.

The third leg is goal: What are you hoping to accomplish? The idea here is to focus on yourself, not how the other person will respond. I love the idea of considering the goal and having it clear in your mind. Your goal in talking to your partner about the mug is to let them know you have a preference and is important to you. Also, there would be more alignment and connection in your relationship and not the distance from something unspoken between you. Even if that unspoken thing is that a part just wants a summer mug in the summertime.

Notice what parts came up as you read about the three-legged stool. Which areas do you have a harder time with? Invite the parts of you who struggle to tell you about this. Check for an open heart or a soft curiosity toward them.

For More Connection Today

 You do have the confidence it takes to address the smallest issues in relationships. Pay attention to parts who reacted above and note their concerns. They have good reason for their fears. Start small to practice, keeping in mind the stool metaphor and being with your parts who have your protection in mind. Ask them: What are they afraid would happen if they did not do their role? Relationships are often are biggest, most complex trailheads.

DAY 22 · *Kindness*

Some relationships are incredibly difficult. It is often hard to remember that the people you are struggling with have parts and Self. I feel this way about "mean people" or "cold people."

My parts often have a strong reaction when they will perceive someone as cold and mean. One part of me will Cut Them Off quickly. I will not even make any eye contact and I will feel numb and disconnected. That is a cue I am blended with a part who is triggered. When I check inside, I hear the parts tell me these types of people are dangerous.

I know my parts are responding to the parts in others. I am not seeing their Self, but their protective system. Their parts have walls and defenses up for reasons that make sense to them. However, knowing this does not help my parts who only sense their protectors and want to hide from what they feel is scary.

Notice what happens inside of you when you have to engage with someone who is difficult. Maybe it is not mean and cold, maybe it is too happy and friendly or selfish and self-focused. Think about the qualities in others that trigger a part's reaction.

Often, you have no choice to have a relationship with that person if they are a co-worker, family member, colleague, or friend of a friend.

What do you do when this is the case? You are at a party, a meeting, or an event and there is someone who rubs you the wrong way or you just do not like them for whatever reason.

A part of me just said, "Am I allowed to not like someone?"

"I think so." Another part says with uncertainty.

I also have a part saying, "Can I write that some people are cold and unkind? Do I need to write it is just parts of them? Do I need to be more precise?"

Another part says, "Why do I have to clarify? I'm going to not like some people and that is okay."

And then I hear, "But if this is true then some people may not like you and that is definitely not okay."

Interesting. See how letting these parts dialogue together when listening with curiosity can get to a deeper level more quickly? By giving protective parts voice they will show you the younger, vulnerable parts they are protecting.

My Need To Like Everyone or see the best in everyone is protecting a part that is afraid of being unliked, unaccepted, unloved. Not only is she afraid of this but she may feel this way about herself. I am curious about this part.

Self connects with this younger part by hearing her fears, letting her know she is loved. Her fears are around following the rules of being nice, being liked, having others see you as good. She tells me, "If I don't like someone, I need to pretend I do. That way I am still seen as nice, and I am liked by everyone."

Do I have to be nice to everyone?

There is a kindness movement in schools, which I very much appreciate. You don't have to be friends with everyone, but you need to be kind. Kind is not the same as nice. Nice feels fake, like your happiness is more important than mine: I have to be nice to you because it will make you feel better.

I notice this part of me who has many protective reasons to be nice. I let her know she does not have to interact with people who trigger her. I can interact with them. I can keep us safe.

Kindness feels like manners with boundaries. I like manners and they were highly valued in my family. Manners and boundaries equal kindness. My parts like this rule. I can be polite and emotionally distant. I don't have to share feelings or be open, yet still can be caring toward another.

Manners and boundaries and kindness.

My parts like these ideas because they provide safety for the parts by having a structure and a guideline in challenging relationships.

For More Connection Today

Who are the difficult people in your life? How do your parts respond when you are around them? What do they want to voice to you right now? How can you be with your parts?

Give yourself permission to be kind and not nice, to have manners and boundaries. How does that feel different for you when you imagine being with other people in a different way? Let your parts say whatever they want and see what fears or concerns may be hidden underneath.

DAY 23 *Voice*

One of the most challenging times in relationships are when my parts act out their feelings instead of allowing me to speak for them. This can look like shutting down and not speaking, slamming cabinet doors, or shoving chocolate cake in my mouth.

We teach kids to use their voice instead of having temper tantrums. The boy throws a Lego dragon across the room instead of saying, "I am frustrated that the leg keeps falling off. Can you help me figure out how to make this work?"

This may trigger a part of me who worries or believes he cannot control his anger because of my own relationship to anger. This part may yell back at him or tell him he is being inappropriate and take away his Legos. This part of mine does not see the part of him who is hurting and frustrated.

Adults do the same thing as kids. Your partner did not do something you wanted him to do so you stomp around, avoid eye contact, pick a fight about something unrelated, or criticize him on a safer topic.

Why don't you just say what is bothering you? This is a fantastic trailhead.

There are a lot of good reasons parts are afraid and hesitant. Maybe parts tell you it will make it worse and they want to keep the peace. Maybe parts tell you they don't like the feeling of conflict and tension because it feels like anxiety and it is scary. Maybe parts tell you that your partner will turn it on you, and you will end up apologizing and feeling guilty.

Explore this avoidance with curiosity, notice any polarization, and have an open heart toward the parts involved in these dynamics. You can see a polarization: some parts want you to speak up and some do not.

Imagine some of your own parts around the relationship and communication table. Who is there?

I have a part who engages in Storytelling. It will tell me a story about why my friend or family member did not do what I wanted them to do. The story is probably:

1) Not fair;
and **2)** Not true.

Other parts tell me a Story about who I am, what I deserve, what I am worthy of, etc., which leads me to not speak up.

Unblending and separating from these parts to get to know them can help me speak from Self and use my voice so I am not acting out my parts' feelings. We value this in children. We need to value it in ourselves.

When I think about a time I did not speak up when I wanted to, I notice my face feels warm and my heart begins to race. I feel fearful. When I focus on the fear, I notice a frozen feeling, like I cannot speak, as if I am having a fight or flight response. I sit with this part, sending her my open heart and compassion. I wait until she notices me and see how she responds to my interest and attention. I listen for what she wants me to know or see.

She may show me other times when I have used my voice and it did not work out well. The other person got mad at me or pressured me to defend my feelings. I regretted saying anything at all.

She may show me how old she is and where she is stuck in place and time. She may think I am very young, too. She may need to be updated, for me to show her who I am and to let her know she is no longer stuck in time.

She may need to be told she does not have to be there when we speak up for ourselves. She does not have to be the one to say anything. I will say something—not my younger, scared part who is triggered. I ask her what she would rather be doing, and she tells me she would rather be roller skating.

I realize stomping around my kitchen is the behavior of a 13-year-old. Of course, she would respond this way. I really get her and understand how and why she shows up. She does not feel heard or seen because of her age and because of the family situation she had growing up.

In Self, I can use my voice and speak for what I need, what I feel, and what my parts are experiencing. I let this part know I've got this; I can be the one involved in speaking up.

For More Connection Today

 Notice the ways you act out your feelings. Check inside to see what story your parts are telling you about the other person and yourself. Practice unblending and giving a voice to your experience. See if there is a younger part acting out, connect with this part and find out what it wants you to know. Ask it how old it is and see if they are stuck in the past. If so, update them with your age and life situation with gentleness and compassion.

DAY 24 · *Connect*

In this last section, we are going to work through an entire healing experience together with one of the parts you have identified over the past few weeks. Begin by choosing one part you are curious about. It could be a part you are feeling right now or it could be a part from earlier in your work.

We want to connect to this part by either imagining the scenario that triggers it or connecting to it by what you are noticing in your body right now. Let's practice with both.

Imagine a time when you felt this part's energy. If it is a critic, imagine a time when you were really calling yourself mean names. If it is anger at your spouse, boss, or child, imagine they did the thing they always do to make you mad. If it is an addicted behavior you do, imagine you are standing at the fridge, at the bar, at the casino, or at the computer. Got it? Are you there?

Now focus on the sensations you are having: Where do you notice it in your body? If you have a thought about it such as, "I think it is dumb and I think I do it because of..." that is a thinking part. We love

these logical, analytical, Figure-It-Out parts. Thank that part for its help and ask it to give you space.

Return your attention back to your body. What else are you noticing? Maybe you notice a fluttering in your chest, tension in your shoulders, uneasiness in your stomach. Put your focus on this sensation.

How are you feeling toward this part? Ask parts to give you space until you notice a curiosity, an open heart toward it. Take your time. You know how to do this. Remind your parts you want to hear from them and you can do that best when they give you space.

See if you can deepen your connection to this part by noticing if there is an image, shape, or color. Notice where it lives in your body.

I am feeling a Critic in my head and I notice a light headache. When I put my attention on it, the feeling increases and I hear, "You can't do anything right!" I see an image of a stern looking Librarian shaking her finger at me.

Or maybe I'm feeling anger at my son. I notice this in my arms and shaking hands. I hear, "He never

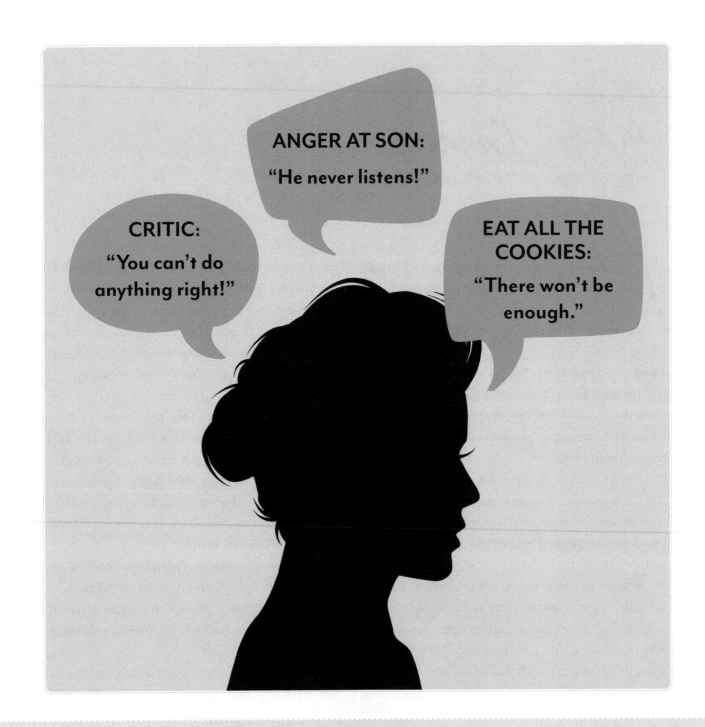

listens!" I feel defeated in my body. I have the urge to disconnect from him and walk into another room.

Or maybe I am feeling the urge to Eat All the Cookies. I notice a feeling of panic in my stomach and an urgency like I'm being pushed forward. I hear, "There won't be enough!" I see only the color gray. I notice a desperate urge to eat all the cookies quickly before I change my mind.

For More Connection Today

 Try this. Take your time. We call this Find, Focus, Feels Toward and Flesh out. Find a part, notice where it is in your body, check to see if your heart is open to it, and ask parts who are not open to give you space. You have been doing pieces of this all along. Smile. Ask parts to step back so you can get a clearer vision of this target part. You got it. Self knows what to do.

DAY 25 *Assure*

We are going to continue your connection to your chosen **target part** by checking in with your body. Where do you experience this part in your body? What sensations are you having? Where does this part live in your body?

Remind it of your feelings of warmth and interest. Notice how you are experiencing this part right now as it is with you.

We want to address any of the fears your other parts may have of going further and meet who it is protecting. Despite that it never looks like this, I imagine this as a line of concerned parts. As they each meet me, they step aside, eventually leading me to the one at the end of the line: the exile.

We want to assure the parts of your presence and safety. Our eye is on the exile. This is where we are heading. We know that to help our protectors we have to help what and who they are protecting. But we can't barrel through. We have to be respectful and assure them of our presence and safety. We want them all to have an experience of Self so they will give space and trust that Self is the best one to take care of the exile.

I have a part who tells me Do Not Ask for things I need and want. It does not want me to ask for help or to reach out to others. If I look at this part with compassion and openness, I hear that it does not think people are reliable and they will think less of you if you ask.

When I stay with Do Not Ask with curiosity, it tells me that it is male and he shows me a little girl who gets bruised easily. He tells me he is her big brother and he cannot trust me with her. I ask why and he says, "You are never around. She needs consistency and I can be that for her."

So to recap what I know so far, my Do Not Ask for things part is a male. He seems to be protecting a younger female part who sees the younger girl as his sister and he does not trust me with her.

He is telling me one important fear: I won't be consistent. I know that consistency and reliability in others is emotional safety for me. What is true on the outside with other people is also true on the inside with my own system.

I tell him I didn't know, and I am here now. I let him feel my love and interest for him and for her.

I ask him what else is he afraid of? He says, "I am worried we will become her entirely. She will take over because her emotions are so big and intense. We couldn't survive if she did."

I let him know I understand that and that is not going to happen. If he lets me meet her, I can help her and he can stay with me while I do. He can interrupt at any point.

He also likes being her big brother and it is a really important job he does not want to lose. He likes his job but admits he is overwhelmed by it and often exhausted. He has to be on the lookout all the time for possible ways "I" will be bruised. That is hard work.

When I ask what else he would like to do, he says he has never thought he could do something else. Just asking this question opens up new ideas for this part and he begins to wonder what he could do with this freedom. I also see him as a little boy who does not want to be in charge of his sister all the time.

But he likes this role—it makes him feel necessary and needed. He also likes how we create a life of protection. He says, "Because you are this way (too sensitive, easily bruised), I have helped you make a life full of loving people. I keep negative drama away from you. You can't handle that."

I thank him! I'm so grateful he has helped me create this kind of life and I don't want that to end. I ask him if we can work together now and reassure him that creating a safe life is still important.

For More Connection Today

Check inside and ask what your protective parts are afraid would happen if they let you closer to the one they are protecting? Listen with compassion. These fears are real and maybe are based on this part's experience.

Before Self was leading, before you were aware you had a Self, these parts have been leading. You are new to them, the idea that you are here and can take the wheel from them may be scary. Of course they are uncertain.

How would you like to address your parts' fears right now? What have you noticed when a part shuts you down? When you wanted to know more about your target part and you felt blank, distracted or shut down?

Ask this part, "What is it afraid would happen if it lets you connect?" Let this part feel you with it and assure it that everyone, including it and the one it is protecting, will feel better if it allows you to proceed.

DAY 26 · *Update*

One of the most important things for our parts to know and feel is your adult leadership. They are no longer stuck in the memories and experience of the past. We call this **Updating.**

Your parts may show you memories. This is their way of telling you how and when they were needed.

Let me give you a few examples. There are times when you react to a situation as if you were much younger. This happened to me when I was cutting up an onion for potato salad with my mom and sister. I began to feel myself shake, I noticed a lot of anxiety and heard the thought, "You aren't going to do this right." I froze.

Right then my sister asked my mom, "How do you want me to cut the potatoes?" My mother said she did not care and it didn't matter to her. My sister replied, "Well, when we were younger you did." My mother laughed and said she was just glad we were together in her kitchen.

I realized my sister and I were having the same experience. We both remembered my mother having strong opinions about how things should be done. But in this moment, I am not with my 30+ year old exhausted mother, I'm actually with my 60+ year old mother, and I am not an angsty preteen. The part of me who is triggered in that moment does not know that.

I can take a deep breath and I can say to the part, "I am here. I totally understand this reaction. Feel my breath with you. Let me be here. You don't have to be."

By having an internal experience that does not match the present external experience, I know a part has been triggered and needs to be updated.

I also notice an urge to eat the plate of chocolate chips cookies my mom just baked. I feel this desire to be alone with these cookies immediately!

One thing is clear to me: a part of me (or many) have used food to soothe myself my entire life. When I focus on this part, even as I am writing this, I hear, "I didn't have another way; I didn't know what else to do. Eating is the only thing I knew to do when I felt upset or unsettled."

My family didn't color (I just had a part say, "Why didn't you just color in a coloring book?") or create. We ate. We still eat. My father comes to visit and we talk about what we are about to eat, what we are eating, what we are eating later. I call him on the phone and he asks me what the plan is for our dinner. We send each other food pictures.

The way I connected to my father was through eating. I loved going to his house every other weekend and eating cold Oreos out of the fridge from a big lettuce Tupperware container. There was no three-cookie-rule in his house. I don't think there were any rules actually.

I let the part who holds shame around eating know that it is an understandable behavior given its role in our childhood. When I am distressed, when I feel like my mom or anyone in the world is mad at me, when I don't feel connected, or when I have any negative emotion at all, a part of me has a great idea of how to help me. Cookies. Eat. All. Of. The. Cookies.

It is the only idea she has and she has been suggesting it for a long time. It is the only way she knows to help.

I connect with her in my body and feel her as a nervous feeling in my stomach. I feel curious about her and tell her this. I ask her how old she thinks I am and she says, "Ten."

First, this age question gives me a lot of information. I may assume the exile is 10 years old. I also may assume this may be a 10-year-old who learned to eat to protect something younger. I have a part that is curious and will ask the part if she can tell us.

Secondly, a lot of healing begins to happen when the part sees and hears from you. You are the adult in the room. You are the resource. You are the one who can help. Your part does not feel so alone anymore.

I have her look at me and see me, see how old I am and how many resources I now have. This may be shocking and hard for her. I stay with this part with comfort and compassion.

She did not know we have a zillion amazing ways to help us feel better. I have so many tools, so many ideas, so many ways to help. But she doesn't know because back then at 10 years old I didn't. I only had my body and food.

I let her know. I update her. I let her feel me with her.

I tell her about yoga and breathing. I tell her about writing. I tell her about prayer and meditation. I tell her she has options. We can pet our dog or play blocks with the boy. I also tell her I got it. She doesn't need to deal with the hard stuff. I am here and I will.

I say, "I don't need you to do that anymore; we aren't in that situation. Thank you for how you protected me back then."

For More Connection Today

As you continue to deepen your relationship with your target part, see what needs to be updated. This can be an ongoing practice you notice as you go throughout your day. Ask the part how old it thinks you are and gently let it know or show it your actual age. Let it feel and experience your Self.

DAY 27 · *Healing*

We are ready to meet who the protector has been protecting. You have already spent time getting to know your protector and building trust.

I return to the protector, the one from yesterday who wants to Eat All the Cookies. I ask her if she will introduce me to the one inside she is protecting.

I practice the skills I have been honing, over and over again. I check in and ask for space from any other parts who come up at this point, the parts who worry about getting overwhelmed or flooded, the parts who are critical of the cookie eater, and the parts who are worried about what we will find out.

I let these parts feel my warmth toward them, my calm presence. I ask them for space. I will continue to check in my body and around my heart to assess for qualities of Self so that the protector and the exile feel me and feel safe.

I return my attention to the one who thinks I am 10 years old, the one who tends to overeat in order to help me deal with emotions. I see this as 2 parts;

Three-year-old

Ten-year-old

1 part eating to protect the feelings of the other. It is like they are twins or two sides of the same coin.

I see a 10-year-old little girl, curled up in a corner. I stand in the room with her. She lets me know that she feels all alone and she this feeling is so intense it feels like she could die. She feels she is supposed to be big enough to handle these changes but she is not! She is still little and this is all very hard.

I check in my heart and notice a part who is annoyed by her, wants her to toughen up! I ask this part for some space and it agrees so I thank it. I turn my attention back to this 10-year-old.

I let her know her fear makes sense because a child would die if left ultimately alone. She would not have food or shelter. She believes she will die from this feeling of loneliness. This explains the intensity in my system when she is triggered.

I check in again and I feel so much love and compassion toward her. I let her know and send this to her. I move closer to her. I feel love toward her and send that love to her. She notices me and feels me with her.

Sometimes there is an actual memory, a scene from your childhood. Sometimes there is just an image of a child. This image does not have to actually be you as you looked when you were younger. Sometimes it is a feeling in your body, an abstract shape or a sensation.

Whatever is coming up, imagine getting close to this part with your compassionate, open heart.

For More Connection Today

It is your turn. Take your time. It is okay if something does not come up right away. Keep an open heart and dialogue with your parts. Let them know you are here and curious.

We want to heal the younger parts so the protectors do not have to work so hard. If we get permission to go to these younger parts and heal them from their burdens, the protectors can find a new role in our system.

DAY 28 *With-ness (witness)*

I hope you were able to identify a younger part in your system which is holding some pain, some memory or experience. We want to imagine going *into* the memory and being with the part in a way it needed. We want to hear from it and want it to feel your attention and presence.

We do not just want to learn about a memory. We want to be in the memory, with the younger part of you who had this experience.

Now, I turn my focus back on the younger part from yesterday. I see a 10-year-old curled up in the corner. I am sitting about three feet away from her on the floor.

I feel curious about her and what she is experiencing, and I let her know. I am letting her know my feelings toward her in order for her to sense me, to sense my Self.

This is important. I stay with this for a bit sending my attention and letting her know my feelings toward her. I want to spend some time here with this young part and sending my compassion to her.

I send this part my open heart and see how she responds. I ask what she wants me to know and just listen. I am with her. I make sure she feels me just being with her.

I invite you to begin to do this. Refocus on the part you identified yesterday. If you feel compassion toward this part, send this to it and see how it experiences that from you. You can ask it how it wants to be together, how far it wants to be from you and where it wants you to be.

As you continue to be with this precious part of your system, finding out about its experience, be with it in a way that it needs. See if it will tell you its story: Where is it in time and place? What are its beliefs and feelings? What does it want you to know about it?

If you become overwhelmed with intense feelings, ask it to pull its energy away from you a bit. Ask it not to flood you. Ask it to come out in front a bit more. Ask it for space so you can be with it. You do not need to feel the feelings of this part in order to be with it and to understand.

My 10-year-old wants me to come closer to her and eventually, wants me to hold her. As she feels my presence and care she no longer feels lonely. I let her know

I will always be with her; I assure her I am not going to leave. She shows me she picked up eating as a strategy at 10, but in our togetherness she melts into a 3-year-old.

My 10-year-old cookie eater is protecting the alone feelings of a 3-year-old. This makes a lot of sense to me knowing my history and I understand the felt sense of the 10-year-old cookie eater and this lonely part hunched in the corner.

Often parts are connected. The aloneness of a 3-year-old is connected to other experiences and parts at ages 10, 13, 17, and 25. I'm noticing other memories popping up from these ages, which have similar themes and feelings.

My 3-year-old part tells me she does not like transitioning from my Dad's house to my Mom's on Sunday nights. My parents have been divorced since I was a baby and I saw my Dad every other weekend. This part carries my distress at leaving my grandmother on Sunday night and the many ways that living in two homes left me unsure of where I belonged. This part is carrying that memory and all its sensations.

I let her know I hear her and I really understand. I am with her in her feelings. I get it! Her feelings make so much sense to me.

She shows me the security blanket she got around this time period in her life to help her feel less lonely. She whispers that nobody knew that was why she had it and why she had it for so long. I let her know she was very resourceful to come up with this plan and I admired how creative she is. She likes that and begins to smile.

The 10-year-old protector and the 3-year-old exile are together. I am holding the 3-year-old. It is more clear to me how they are related. I let the 3-year-old know I see how brave and strong and smart she is even though she did not want to be.

I understand the 3-year-old needed the security blanket to help with her aloneness and the 10-year-old used food to help with the 3-year-old's feelings.

I let them both know they are smart and brave. We sit together; both of them leaning on me, feeling heard, and seen, less ashamed.

For More Connection Today

Be with your younger part in the way it needs you to be, sending it your care, curiosity, compassion, and see how it responds. See if it will tell you its story. Be there with it in the way it needed someone to be at that time.

DAY 29 — *Invitation*

I hope you have felt the benefit of being with a younger part of you and experienced lightness in all areas of your life. There is one more important step we need to take. We want to ask this part if it is ready to come to the present.

I bring my attention back to the 3-year-old Lonely One and the 10-year-old Cookie Eater who protects her. I show this little girl what my life is like right now. In my current life, I rarely feel lonely. I have lot of friends and a great family who I feel connected to emotionally, even though they are physically far away.

I ask her if she is ready to leave the place she is in and come into the present. She can go wherever she wants to go. She can be with me in my house, she can go to a park in my town, she can go to Disneyworld, or she can go to an imaginary place. She can come into my heart or come stand right next to me. It does not matter as long as it is in the present and she knows my Self energy is always with her. I assure her even when I am doing all the other things I do in my life, she always has access to me. I am not going anywhere.

My 3-year-old wants to sit on the floor in the middle of my kitchen playing with dolls. This way she can look up to me as I move around life and be in the midst of family routines.

I ask her what she wants to let go of, what she wants to unload, and what she wants to release from the past. This may be old feelings and beliefs she held. This may be ways she felt in her body. She states she wants to let go of feeling lonely and the feeling that something is wrong with her.

I ask how she wants to do that using one of the elements: light, ground, air, water, fire. I invite her to imagine sending it up in the air, the birds taking it away. Or burying it in the ground, giving nourishment to plants. Or sending it out into the water, floating far out to sea. Or into the light, turning it into something pure. Or, burning in a fire, ashes rising up into the sky.

Your young part will know how it wants to release its burdens and will come up with its own way of doing it. You may be delighted and surprised at how creative

your parts can be at this. You also may be surprised at how quickly this happens.

My 3-year-old wants to put her burdens far out to sea on a boat that looks like a duck. We do this together and she feels a lot of joy.

Then I ask what she qualities she would like to invite in now that there is more room and space inside her. She wants to have more play and more freedom to play. I smile, validate this makes a lot of sense, and say she can have exactly that. I play with her along that beach as she takes in and experiences this play and this freedom.

I check back with my 10-year-old to make sure she saw what happened with the 3-year-old. She says did and wants to join on the play by roller skating around the 3-year-old so we can all be in the kitchen together. I see them both in my kitchen, the 3-year-old feeling light and connected to me. She is playing with her dolls and enjoying the silliness of the 10-year-old who is roller skating around her.

I check back with all the protectors who were watching over these two to see if they saw what happened and how they are. They feel calm and I ask them what they want to do now. They say they want to help us connect to my husband, family, and friends. They want to make fun plans so we will not be lonely. They find this creative and exciting, not urgent or stressful. I let them know this is a great idea, and I would love their help.

For More Connection Today

 Have your part notice what it feels like to not carry the burden any longer in their body. They often will notice spaciousness. Ask what they would like to have more of, what they would like to invite in and they will often say play or rest with a specific idea of what they want to do. Encourage it to invite in qualities it wants more of inside. Continue to let it know you are with them through this process. And you will be with them now always, even when you are busy with other things in life. Have them notice what this new feeling is like.

Check back in with your protective parts, all the parts who gave you space to connect with this young one. See if they noticed what happened and the shift in this younger part. Ask if they also notice a shift in themselves, too. Thank them for allowing you to heal her. Celebrate with them and let them know you will continue to connect with all of them.

Feel the difference in your body. Notice these steps: bring into present, unburden beliefs and feelings to an element with a ritual and invitation. This usually happens quite quickly that is why I put all these sweet gifts into one day. It may seem a lot for one day, but it can happen quite quickly.

Make an intention to check in with this precious part for the next 30 days and decide together what this will look like. My parts like an early morning check-in before I open my eyes. They like knowing I will talk with them in therapy and I will journal with them. They may like being drawn or using art in some way to represent them externally. If I wake up in the middle of the night, I spend that time with them. Check and see how your parts want to stay connected with you.

Ask them if they feel complete.

DAY 30 · *Appreciation*

You did it! Today is the final word in this process and you may notice parts of you having some feelings. How do you typically do endings? I invite you to let your parts know you can do this ending differently. Some parts may be excited and tell you, "You finished something! You didn't put it down halfway through, give up or forget! Yay!"

Other parts may be a bit nervous and say, "Well, what do we do now? I just started on this and now what?"

Right now, pause, listen inside and see who is here. You know how to do this now. Listen for words in your mind, sensations in your body, and feelings in and around you. Who is up, who wants to communicate something?

You are now familiar with how your parts communicate. Notice this. The ability to notice is in you now. You cannot unknow this now. You may forget to check in with your parts, but you can always return to noticing and acknowledging them with each new breath.

Let them know you are here. You have been here all along and you will continue to be here. Smile.

Send them appreciation for all the work they have done for you throughout your life, not just over the past 30 days. Let them know you are grateful and in awe of how hard they have protected you and have fought for you. Your parts—all of them—are completely and utterly on your side.

How does that feel inside? Check in with your body. Who wants to speak to you right now? Let them know you feel that toward them and see how they react. Be with whatever and whoever shows up. You know how to do this. *Self knows.*

You know when a part is driving the bus. Focus on that part. How does it present itself? Check for Self by asking how you feel toward it. Keep asking for space from other parts, assessing Self by looking for those C qualities. Once Self shows up, unblend, and befriend. Get to know this part and address its fears and concerns. Ask it to show you what it is protecting.